Terry Cooper

Terence Robert Cooper was born one foggy October day in the Borough of Dagenham, on the banks of the polluted Thames. He was an ordinary submissive working class schoolboy until he was 13 years old, when a "near death experience" changed his entire attitude towards life. He had contracted Hepatitis A and had been given up as lost by the doctors when he realised life was meant to be lived to the full.

On his recovery, and well in advance of his time, he quickly became a rebel against conformity, formulating his personal motto, "In the kingdom of the blind, the one eyed is quickly put to death because he is different."

A whole series of unforeseen events was to lead him into a parallel world of Nazism, aristocracy, millionaires and mystics, where he was able to adapt himself to situations which he had never dreamt existed while he was a schoolboy in Dagenham.

Mastering the language which he once detested at school he has now lived in France for 44 years, marrying a Belgian woman at the late age of 33 and recently becoming a grandfather, "the last step before the old folks' home."

Still refusing to accept conformity, Terry continues a clandestine life of wild adventures.

Death
by
Dior

Terry Cooper

Dynasty
Press

Dynasty Press Ltd.
36 Ravensdon Street
London SE11 4AR

www.dynastypress.co.uk

First published in this version by Dynasty Press Ltd.

ISBN: 978 0 9568038 6 3

Copyright © Terry Cooper 2013

Cover Artwork from a design by Rupert Dixon.
Typeset by Shore Books, Blackborough End, Norfolk.

Printed and bound in the United Kingdom.

"One stone in the middle of a road can change the entire destiny of a nation."

Napoléon Bonaparte

To my grandson Jackinson

If Christian Dior had not decided to renovate a disused water mill in Milly-la-Forêt,
you would not be here today.

Contents

Interview with Françoise Dior on French television

An interview with Françoise Dior, given to Jacques Chattard, the London correspondent of the *"Journal Télévisé d'ORTF"*, at the Coventry home of Colin Jordan, "World Führer" of the World Union of National Socialists. Broadcast on the 2nd October 1963.

J.C.   Miss, how did this Franco-British romance begin?

F.D.   Well, I saw an article in *France-Soir* (second widest distributed newspaper in France) where it was a question of the movement of Colin Jordan and of himself, I was very enthusiast being a National Socialist for a long time and I wrote to him, he did not reply himself because he did not know French, but he made a reply (by someone) and afterwards I took a plane and I went to see him.

J.C.   And when did he ask you to marry him?

F.D.   He asked me to marry him in the plane which was taking us to France, not long ago, twenty days ago, between England and France over the Channel. It is symbolic for the World Union of National Socialists.

J.C.   Do you share the national ideas, Facist, of your husband?

F.D.   Not Fascist, National Socialist, oh yes, certainly.

J.C.   Since a long while?

F.D.   Consciously, oh yes, since several years, but finally, unconsciously I always have been.

J.C.   When you are married will you be a housewife or will you share the political activities of your husband?

F.D.   Oh, I will participate in his political activities, I am not at all a housewife.

J.C.   And that will take which form?

F.D.   Well, my exact position, I represent the countries of French expression. That means for the international question, not at all for the English question.

J.C.   Do you think this will give you a lot of work?

F.D.   A certain work, yes.

J.C.   Do you have many adherents in France?

F.D.   A certain number, but finally we do not seek to reach the masses. We seek to form an executive.

J.C.   An elite?

F.D.   That's it. We have it.

J.C.   Eventually, are you ready to follow your husband into prison?

F.D.   Of course.

J.C.   Have you the intention to have children, to have a family when you are married?

F.D.   As much as possible.

J.T.   Will you bring the children up in the principles of National Socialism?

F.D.   Of course.

J.C.   Can you explain what this consists of?

F.D.   That consists of, firstly, in my opinion, to keep the race pure, not to marry, evidently, someone who is not of the Aryan race; to fight for National Socialism, that means, how can I say it, yes, defend your race.

J.C.   Is it.........

F.D.   Venerate the Fuehrer. Adapt National Socialism to our actual times, that means each Aryan of the entire world to be a combatant, not simply for Germany. It is our Holy Land like Palestine is the Holy Land for the Jews and Christianity.

J.C.   Will you teach your children, for example, the hatred of Jews?

F.D.   It is not exactly hatred; we do not want them in our home (land), that's all.

J.C.   What is your ideal "hero type"?

F.D.   The Fuehrer.

J.C.   Can you explain better?

F.D.   Adolf Hitler.

J.C.   Miss, have you fixed the date for your marriage?

F.D.   Yes, next Saturday.

J.T.   And where will it take place?

F.D.   Well, Coventry for the civil marriage and afterwards we will go to London where there will be a National Socialist ceremony, in the rites of our race, the ancient Aryan.

J.C.   And exactly what does this consist of?

F.D.   It is a bit complicated to explain, there is the incision of a finger, our blood will be mixed, and we kiss a blank page of *Mein Kampf*................................

End of recording.

Source:www.atlantico.fr/pepitesvideo/l-union-francoise-dior-avec-nazi-anglais-46171.html

CHAPTER 1

Prologue: Early years

Standing on the seafront at Calais, I am looking across the Channel towards an England from which I am exiled and which I shall never set foot on again for the rest of my life. It is a sunny day, the ferries are passing backwards and forwards, and on the sands some children are happily digging sandcastles, lost in the oblivion of their innocence.

Mine is the oblivion of experience. I remember my own childhood, digging these same castles in the sands at Walton-on-the-Naze, and am overwhelmed with a sudden wave of nostalgia. How on earth did a little scruff, born one misty autumn day in Chadwell Heath, a direct descendant of the East London ragged schools, become a British Nazi, frequenter of French aristocrats and millionaires, finish up married with a Belgian girl, comfortably retired and officially dead, living on the banks of the Seine, south of Paris, unable to return to my native Dagenham?

Maybe our lives are exactly the same as the binary computer and from the beginning to the end we are continually faced with the alternative, yes or no? Do we make things happen, do we choose to let them happen? Sometimes pleased with the result, believing we are in control, while at other times the result can be catastrophic and we take ourselves to be the victims; when in reality and with afterthought, certain events could have been avoided if only we had made the right choice at the time on hand. The path to exile, which I followed from my grandparents' house in Morley Road where I was born, to my present apartment and shadowy sepulchre in Evry, via Paris, Nice, Vienna, Munich, Jersey, Normandy, and Fontainebleau has certainly presented me with some very extreme choices.

Right from the start, I was a rebel. I hated school, not because I was averse to learning, on the contrary, I learnt to read and write at the age of three. This precociousness immediately put me outside the stereotyped system, where little boys were expected to crawl about on the floor pushing a wooden fire engine or a boat on wheels while the little girls were crammed into a canvas house in one corner of the classroom to change the nappies of their dolls. I wanted books to read but our spinster old maid teacher scolded me by insisting that "We" don't read yet. This perpetual "We" made my early years a misery every time I dared step out of line, something I just could not help myself from doing, either intentionally or by omission.

My earliest memory of this class, painful at the time, makes me laugh today. My best friend, Phillip Denis, had the audacity to creep over to the girls' corner, a heinous offence in itself, where he poked one of the eyes out of Linda's dolly. Hauled out in front of the entire class Miss treated him as if he had been the assassin I would become. Laughing my head off at his plight, I was hauled out beside him to share the leg slapping. We sat down on the bare floorboards together, crying on each other's shoulders. I was very sorry the day he moved away to Romford.

Few people remain in Dagenham if they can help it and it

was not long before the other member of my "Gang of Three", Derek Ellard, moved away to Ilford. Fortunately two other hardened adventurers started school in the months which followed, John McEwen and David Harris. We stayed together right up until the final days at secondary school. John went to live in Canada shortly after leaving school; while David, who shared most of my insane misadventures, would probably prefer to forget them today as he became a respectable citizen. Many years later I watched the film by Pink Floyd, *The Wall*, and thought, "That's just about as close as you can get to post-war school in Britain during the 50's." Fear of being "different" was the predominant element and it was during these years that I first formulated my proverb, "In the kingdom of the blind, the one eyed is quickly put to death because he is different."

The lessons I came to hate the most were French and History. It was not always so. In junior school I loved history and could re-live every event in my mind, with myself taking part, from Caesar landing in the South, to the Battle of Trafalgar. The unfortunate part was Guy Fawkes. Although I was not a Catholic, I always saw myself down in the cellars of Parliament helping him to stack barrels of gunpowder. Secondary school shattered all that. Our history teacher was a Welsh thug who would thrash about with a billiard cue throughout his lessons, bringing it down on your table within millimetres of your fingers if he thought you were daydreaming, which I invariably was. One night some hero broke into the school, trashed the history room, and snapped the billiard cue in two. The result was devastating. Taff completely lost his head, while the stump gained extra swish.

One lad, Jim Brewster, spent his entire school life daydreaming, like me. He wanted to become a guitarist and was gifted but extremely slow on the uptake. He managed to get his 'O' levels; it was simply a question of the speed at which things registered in his head. One day some school inspectors were doing the rounds, carrying out a survey asking everyone what they wanted to do when they left school. You had a choice in those days and very few people chose the dole. I told Jim there were house points for original answers, so I gave him a few hints and made certain he had memorised them. The inspectors were long forgotten when, right in the middle of one of Taff's lessons, the door opened and, oh horrors, in they walked. Wishing the floor would open up and swallow me, I tried to catch Jim's eye; but no one ever turned round during one of Taff's lessons. Their mission explained, the inspectors started going round the class. The usual answers came out, "I want to work in Ford's," "I want to join the police," "I want to do this, that and the other etc." Then it came to Jim's turn.

"And what do you want to do?"

"I want to be a monk, sir."

Everyone knew better than to dare laugh but I wanted to laugh so hard I felt like being sick. Taff was turning scarlet and you could hear his teeth grinding. The inspectors looked a bit startled but they continued, "And what is your second choice?" The room started going black around me.

"I want to be the call boy at the Windmill Theatre, sir."

I couldn't stand it any longer and told Taff that I'd fallen over in the playground and hit my head against a step. Could I nip down to the cloakroom? He grunted and made a gesture towards the door, so I made my escape before the fireworks started. Just before four o'clock, and after he'd wrung the confessions out of everyone, Taff caught up with me. I thought he would shake me to pieces. Fortunately it was near the end of term so I had the holidays to get over it.

On our first day in our new school our class teacher had given us the timetable for the term. There was a general gasp. "Oh boy! We're going to learn French." That was something completely unimaginable and exotic for Dagenham but, as from the very first lesson, "Oh boy," immediately degenerated into, "Oh Christ!"

Our French teacher was a vicious old woman who we had to address as Madame Julien. I calculated she had married a Frenchman during the war and he had run off and left her. That might not have been the case but at least it was a reasonable explanation for her behaviour. Eight and a half years after my first day in her class, when I arrived at the Gare du Nord, I had not been in Paris one hour before I realised she knew absolutely nothing about France and even less about the language she was supposed to have been teaching us. For three years I managed to endure her violence, until we were given the option of lessons to prepare for our 'O' levels. I struck history and French off my list, although without trying I was always amongst the top three in French.

Towards the end of the third year we had a new headmaster, Mr Woods. I got on very well with him. "Woody" was a dreamer like me, except his dream must have been that he was headmaster of Harrow School. He revived the old school uniform and just to please him some of us started to wear black blazers and grey flannels. A few even went so far as to wear the school tie but we all drew the line about wearing the school crest. At home I always threw my blazer over the end of my bed and my tabby cat used to go to sleep on it. When he moulted I went to school resembling a walking teddy bear, which always upset "Woody". There were some days when I could not stand Mme Julien any longer and on one occasion she sent me down to get the whack for insolence. I managed to talk "Woody" out of it. I think he felt sorry for me. He must have felt sorry for her estranged husband too and the conversation turned towards foreign countries and eventually, the navy, his favourite topic. I spent the rest of the afternoon in his study chatting about ships and the sea.

Going to sea was my dream and I eventually managed to get a place in the school for marine radio officers in the merchant navy when, after five long agonising years, I finally left Lymington Road Secondary Modern.

CHAPTER 2

Sexual education

If my secondary education was of a secondary nature, my sexual education can only be called a great success. It was rapid and I learnt the maximum in the minimum of time. In those days the basic social driving forces were work and sex. Hope played only a minor role. It all began when I was 11, when one of the weirdest families imaginable came to live next door.

The previous tenants had been an old couple who had won the council estate prize each year for the past ten years for the best kept front garden, with hundreds of flowers and a billiard table lawn. This new family transformed it into a barren desert within less than two months after arriving.

A makeshift pantechnicon van dating back to the 30's and the days of moonlight flits pulled up one Saturday morning and the first thing to tumble out of the back were the three kids, John, who was the eldest at 10, David, his younger brother of 9, and eight year old Susan. They were followed by some furniture which normal people in a refugee camp would use as firewood; and the van drove off. The father, Wally, had gone to the local shops for some fish and chips, which he spread out on their table made of an old door laid out on trestles in the back kitchen. One bag came open with the chips falling off onto the floor and Wally snapped to David, "That's yours, down there."

Their family nickname was "Acid" and it really annoyed Wally whenever anyone called them that. Written down on paper their correct name was Adshead, but Acid was the way they pronounced it themselves. They had a strange way of speaking. Chadwell Heath would come out as "Shabbel'if", and the board game of Monopoly was best interpreted as "Bin'opli". They were all short and dead skinny but the strangest of all was their mother. At 11, I was already taller than her; she had long dark hair, dark brown eyes, and dark hairs growing on every visible part of her body. She resembled a human spider. No one ever got to know her real name. To us she was always "Old Mother Acid", or if anyone addressed her she was affectionately called "You." This was Wally's fault; nobody had ever heard him call her anything else. "'Ere "You", wes me car keys? Ere "You", wes me dinner?" and, when he got angry with the kids, "'Ere "You", wes me belt?"

The kids went to the local school and as time passed we grew used to them and their funny ways. Summer or winter their front door was always left wide open. We used to say it was either to let the flies in or to let the stink out. There was no need to knock on the door; any one could walk in as they wished and, on top of everything, were always welcome, not that many people took the risk of being asphyxiated. I loved those flies in the sitting room and could spend hours swatting at them with my ping-pong bat; until one day I hit the light bulb which hung from bare wires just off centre of the room. All the lights in the houses were off centre because the Becontree Estate was on gas until just before the war and had only recently been converted to electricity, leaving the original gas installations in place. At the same time the lamp standards in the street were left on gas until much later. I had to buy a new light bulb out of my pocket money but all I could afford was a 25 watt which made the room look more like a dungeon than ever.

To us boys, Susan was a godsend. Before her arrival we had a great game of "hospitals" going on down the street. We boys were the doctors while the girls were our patients, except for one girl who insisted on being a nurse and who would prepare our patients before we examined them. Remembering the way she handled them I am certain she must have grown up to be a lesbian. The game came to an end when one of the mothers discovered an abnormal amount of earth in her daughter's knickers. Mud was our universal medicine and ice lolly sticks were our scalpels. A confession was beaten out of the girl and the word immediately spread amongst the mothers. When the fathers came home from work that evening it was the night of the great thrashing. From what I heard later, the girls got it worse than the boys and from then on they tended to avoid our games. We were taking no risks with Susan. Any parents who chanced to look out of the window would only see a harmless game of hide and seek in the street. What they never noticed was that Susan changed partners throughout the game, that Susan and her partners always hid in the same place, and that Susan and her partners were always the last to be discovered.

Our main distraction was the Saturday morning pictures at the Odeon at Becontree Heath. Our small group would set out early in the morning and slowly grow in number as we approached the cinema. The basic entry fee was 6d but kids with no brothers or sisters or kids whose fathers worked at Ford's might get a whole shilling if they were lucky. Two of the older girls made it their business to collect up everyone's money. This was my first introduction to communism. They set aside 6d for each member of the group, counted out the price of one ice cream between two for the interval, and then spent the remainder on sweets in the shop opposite the cinema which were shared out just before we went in.

The boys had a different preoccupation: we were working out the sequence in which we would sit next to Susan. The routine was that she would sit in the centre of the row with a string of boys on either side. As soon as the lights went down there was always a volley of apple cores and general rubbish flying in the direction of the screen. The lights would go up and the manager came onto the stage threatening that if ever someone threw something again he would close the cinema for good. When he had finished his speech, which we all knew off by heart, the lights would go down again and this was the indication for the boys immediately beside Susan to go to work. After a reasonable time the two boys would then get up while the line on either side would all move down one seat. The first two took their places at the vacant ends, impatiently waiting for their second turn.

Wally worked for a French polishing firm somewhere in the Mile End Road, restoring the parquet floors of rich clients in the West End. Very often, at the weekend, he would use his old van to bring home some of the clients' furniture, which he would renovate using the products that he had filtered off on the side from work and which helped him round off his pay packet. One week he brought home packing cases each evening, which he piled up in the back garden. At first we thought he might be thinking of emigrating to Australia, as another neighbour who had stocked cases in his garden had done a few months earlier, but on Saturday morning he smashed them up into planks and spent the rest of the day constructing a shed at the end of his garden. The end product would have been considered uninhabitable in any shanty town but Wally was pleased with his work and stood back to admire his handicraft. In the evening as soon as he went out to somewhere or another all the boys poured into it, dragging Susan along with us. John and David were content to sit in the garden with a slice of bread and thinly spread jam without margarine which someone had the kindness to bring along for them. From now on, with a secret den like that, we had no need to play hide and seek in the street any more.

One evening Wally must have come home from work earlier than usual because, while Susan was standing on her upturned orange box holding her dress up to her shoulders with her knickers around her ankles, Wally came crashing through the door. It was pandemonium, with half the boys scrambling off down the garden and through Wally's house while the other half jumped over the fence to escape through mine. Unbelievably, there was no repercussion, as with the night of the great thrashing, so it was only a few days before everything was back to business as usual with Susan.

Time had passed since the Acids had first arrived next door and by now I had started preparing for my 'O' level examination. We had a choice of subjects, which left us a fair amount of spare time between lessons and on top of that I was a school prefect which meant that during the periods without lessons I could wander in and out of school as I chose. In view of the fact that I lived only a few hundred yards from the building, I spent most of my free time at home. One afternoon there was a particularly interesting program on the schools' television that I wanted to see, but our set had broken down and the repair man had not been along yet. I wandered into the Acids' house. There was nobody about, so I switched on their set and sat down on the sofa somewhere between the hole to the left and the spring which poked through at the other end. Old Mother Acid, or rather "You", appeared from out of nowhere and sat down beside me without saying a word. After a while she suddenly sat up straight and whispered, "You mustn't get rude with Susan."

I knew exactly what she meant but this was the first time I had ever heard her speaking this way and it put me completely off my guard. Normally she always squawked like a parrot but now she was almost purring like a kitten. As a reflex and without even thinking I replied, "Did the boys get rude with you when you were a girl?" I immediately clapped my hands over my mouth wishing the sofa would open up and swallow me down the hole.

She remained silent for what seemed to be an eternity then, without bothering to look at me, took my hand and led me out of the sitting room down the passage to the front door. At first I thought she was going to throw me out but instead, still holding my hand, she closed it. This was the first time I had ever seen that door closed in the four years they had lived there. She then led me up the stairs beside the door into the front bedroom which overlooked the street. The entire room was worse than threadbare. There was the standard council house built-in wardrobe over where the stairs might be, a double bed in the centre of the room with a wooden kitchen chair on either side, while a table similar to the one in the kitchen stood under the window. There were piles of clothes everywhere which you had to step over in order to advance into the room. "You" undressed me, then undressed herself, guiding me towards the bed. I was physically shaking like a leaf, not through fear but through expectation. "You" remained silent all the time, while I experienced the worst case of floppy dick I have ever suffered in my life. After a while she began to do something between her legs and I was such a dummy I had no idea what she was up to. She suddenly became stiff all over, half sat up, and then fell back with her eyes only half open and without breathing. Her usual swarthy complexion had turned as white as a sheet and I was terrified she was dead, but finally she opened her eyes and told me to get dressed. As we were going down the stairs she said, "Don't worry; it will be better next time."

So, there was going to be a next time! I floated down the remainder of the stairs and remember nothing which might have happened afterwards. I was in a dream. The next day, instead of doing my homework, I sat glued to the window waiting for John, David, and Susan to come home from school. As soon as they had finished their meal of bread and fish paste they were out in the street playing and I knew the only way they would be back inside again was when Wally came home from work and chased them around the cars with his belt in his hand. I nipped in, gave "You" a hand with the washing up, then we went up to our love nest.

Although she had no breasts, I had discovered "You" was exotic and beautiful; in my eyes she no longer resembled a spider. Even Susan's puffy little mounds were larger than "You"'s breasts, which explained the fact there was never a bra on their washing line each Monday morning. The days passed and "You" was the perfect teacher that any youngster could possibly hope of finding. She taught me very nearly everything imaginable that a youngster should know about a

19

woman's body and, most important of all, she taught me how to please a woman with words and gestures alone, long before having any physical contact. She was a naturally born mistress in the art of love. In return I even taught "You" a few things. The Valence library had an extensive collection of books on sexuality and sexual deviation and I had learnt them all off by heart years earlier, well before the time I was thirteen. Theory had now given way to practice.

My days of bliss passed slowly and sweetly up until one Saturday morning when I was out in the garden feeding my goldfish. There were only two ponds in our street so, whenever someone won a goldfish in a plastic bag at the fairground, it inevitably found its way into my pond for safe-keeping. I had long ago forgotten how many there might be, but as the years passed they started breeding and every spring a new shoal would appear from the depths. I heard "You" spluttering and gurgling in her kitchen and cursing Wally by every name under the sun. He must have found out about our romance and was strangling her. I leapt over the fence to save my precious "You". I found her alone and doing her best to vomit into the kitchen sink. That Friday evening Wally had brought home a set of chairs to polish and had left his mixture of shellac dissolved in alcohol, which he had taken from work, standing on the kitchen table in an old Tizer bottle. When "You" came down to prepare the breakfasts she thought it was a bottle of soda which someone had forgotten to put away and had taken a generous swig.

From then on I decided Wally had to go. I would be 16 in October and free to marry my "You". We would live happily ever after, down by the sea at Walton-on-the-Naze. She could stand on the Naze green at the top of the cliffs, watching for my ship to come in from the ocean, while John and David could go out to work to keep her while I was away. The only thing standing in my way was Wally. Assassination as means of achieving an end had not come into my mind yet at this early age, so I took to praying. Each morning I would lie in bed patiently waiting until I heard Wally start his old van at 8 o'clock precisely. He must have had a good battery because it always took over a hundred turns of the key before the engine spluttered into life. Then he chugged noisily up the road on three cylinders which was my signal to jump out of bed, go down on my knees and begin my prayers. I begged the Lord to help Wally get into a road accident, preferably at Stratford Broadway where the traffic was at its heaviest and preferably a head-on collision with a fully laden lorry on its way to the docks. I promised in return I would go to Sunday school every week for the rest of my life.

One day the Lord did answer my prayers. One of my favourite programmes on the radio was Saturday Club, which followed on after Children's Favourites. Each week they played pop music and had a different visiting group for the morning. At about 10.30am there was a news flash. A number 25 bus had jumped the pavement at Becontree Broadway, killing a shopper in front of a chemist's shop. I knew the shop well, it was P.C. Geddes. Wally had gone out at his usual time with his shopping bags but had failed to return that morning. I could see him completely flattened out against the shop front with his intestines sprawling over the bonnet of the bus and his severed head on the driver's lap. I praised the Lord then dashed out the back to comfort my poor "You". I leapt over the fence and came face to face with Wally, sitting on his back step polishing a bedside cabinet. I congratulated him on his narrow escape then slunk off home over the fence. The Lord had made a mess of the job but, after all, nobody's perfect. Next Monday at school "Woody" stood up after the assembly had finished and said, "You all know what happened this Saturday. If I hear of anyone talking about it, they'll find themselves in my study!" He then raised his arm and brought it down as if he was giving someone the whack. That was the nearest you could get to psychological counselling in the 60's and we were none the worse off for it either.

Just as my 'O' levels were approaching my clandestine romance suffered a severe setback when Wally was unexpectedly made redundant. Some idiot by the name of Cyril Lord had the bright idea of bringing the illusion of affluence to the hard-working, laborious masses by introducing them to a new fashion in housewares. His scam was to manufacture wall-to- wall tufted carpeting using sweat-shop labour in Northern Ireland, then distributing it by means of locally recruited agents working on a commission basis placed in every street throughout the land. This way he counted on having maximum profits with a minimum initial outlay. His sales pitch was, "This is luxury you can afford by Cyril Lord." Cyril must have also economised on his market research because the lino-clad floors of the working classes were far from ready for his carpets and his slogan rapidly disintegrated into, "This is bankruptcy you can afford by Cyril Lord."

Right from the start there was an unexpected side effect which poisoned my romance with "You". The East End and sprawling suburbs ignored his magnificent floor coverings but the West Enders, who had rich friends abroad, were all familiar with continental "moquette" styled carpeting and decided to give it a try for themselves. Although these sales never quite met Cyril's hopes and expectations, they did greatly cripple the French polishing industry. Instead of being renovated, the parquet floors began to find themselves being hidden under the same carpeting which now put Wally out of work. Notwithstanding his new social status, he must have enjoyed his newfound life of leisure because he never tried looking for another job. He would start his day in his old armchair, staring at a blank television screen with a copy of yesterday's Daily Mirror draped across his knees, waiting for the schools' programs to start. He sat there all day, right up until the epilogue and God Save the Queen, before switching off and finally going to bed. My romance with "You" was reduced to furtive kisses, cuddles, and mutual masturbation in the kitchen; with the rare opportunity to slip into bed only on Wednesday and Friday mornings, when Wally was obliged to go down to the labour exchange to sign on for his dole.

The whole street was just beginning to wonder how he managed to keep his family when the surprise of a lifetime occurred. One morning I went in through the perpetually open front door and found myself standing on a thick red carpet running the length of the passage while the same carpeting climbed up the stairs beside me. I felt as if I was in Buckingham Palace. It must have all been installed some time during the night because I never noticed anything exceptional arriving during the day. In the sitting room the floor was covered by an enormous Persian carpet, the old sofa and armchairs had given way to a matching three piece suite, while in one corner stood the latest model of a radiogram, the marvel of a combined radio and record player all in one cabinet. To crown everything the room was dominated by a massive 24 inch screen television set. "You" and the kids all had new clothes with "You" now wearing pale violet panties, while Susan had gained a Junior

Miss bra. Only Wally remained dressed as if he was a rag and bone man in his usual creased grey striped suit one size too large for him and his collarless shirt. At least he shaved regularly.

The neighbours were all mystified and the only explanation which was given during the continual interrogations which followed was that Wally had won the pools. Nobody believed them. Each Saturday evening, when the paper boy cycled down the street calling out, "Classified," neither John nor David had ever joined the queue of kids clutching a three penny bit to buy the newspaper which would decide if the family was suddenly worth the magic figure of £75,000 or not. (A house in those days would have cost less than one thousand). There was a secret somewhere, but the Acids remained as silent as the grave.

One Saturday morning, while I was feeding my goldfish I looked up to Susan's bedroom to find there were no curtains up at the window. It was the same with John and David's room. I jumped over the fence and the back door was locked. I peered into the curtainless kitchen window and the entire room was empty. I ran out to the front, where the door was equally locked, only to find the sitting room had no curtains and the room was as bare as the kitchen. I rushed back through our house into the garden to fetch our apple tree ladder and began to climb up the front of the house to "You"'s bedroom, when one of the neighbours came up behind me and asked what I was doing. My love nest was as bare as the rest of the house and all I could say between my tears was, "The Acids have gone." I was heartbroken. This was my very first *chagrin d'amour*. He took a look himself to make certain, then went off to spread the news.

During the weeks which followed there was a steady stream of bailiffs, tally men and debt collectors going from door to door, asking if anyone knew the Acid's new address; but nobody knew of their whereabouts. Come to think of it, nobody knew where they came from either.

CHAPTER 3

After school

With Lymington behind me, I was now on my first step towards the sea. The entry formalities to my new school were simple enough, but I resented the fact that I was obliged to pay ten shillings to join the students' union. It smacked of the "We" which I had hated throughout my previous school life. I considered myself perfectly capable of expressing myself if needs be without the aid of any socialist "bruvvers" and that becoming a forced "lefty" was out of keeping with a ship's officer's position. All that accomplished, I began to make new friends while at the same time I began learning the basics of technical electricity and the Morse code. There was only one thing which I was afraid might pose a threat to my future career on oil tankers in the Middle East. I chose that option because tankers had the highest pay together with added risk premiums. Prancing about in a ballroom on passenger liners could wait for the time being. The problem was the fact that I did not know how to swim. Very few in my class at Lymington had ever learnt and this was not surprising, because, although we had swimming classes every Thursday morning, they began at 8.30am in the open air baths in Valence Park with a temperature very often inferior to 10°C.

Before my first year had finished I had become the school expert on how to avoid swimming lessons. The register was called once the class had returned to school and my favourite ploy was to stay in bed late, wet my hair before leaving home and then hide in a convenient front garden while waiting for the column to pass along Bonham Road on the route from the park to the school. At the right moment I would pop out, join the column and march along with my damp towel under my arm as if I had been present from the very beginning. Otherwise I knew every possible hiding place in the school building, and there were more of them than you can imagine. A quick visit to the cloakroom to wet my hair was all that was needed. In the end the others came to me for advice about avoiding swimming.

Most of my ancestors had been to sea before me, including my great-grandfather and his two sons. Even his wife's maiden name was Drake. Before the first war my grandfather had sailed a New Zealand line and, at the outbreak, was daft enough to volunteer for minesweepers in the North Sea, one of the most dangerous jobs going at the time. Their sister volunteered to become a Wren. Again, during the second war women were not conscripted but my mother broke the naval line by volunteering for the Royal Artillery, although she was not a very good soldier. Unlike my grandfather, whose record sheet was always stamped as having exceptionally good conduct, she was continually in trouble for being AWL, absent without leave, especially when she was posted to Ulster, a rebel.

Even great-great-grandfather Isaac Gosden and his wife Esther decided to uproot from their native Transylvania during the bloodthirsty purges of the emperor Franz-Josef to settle down in the tranquil little village of Chertsey. I wish I knew why they arrived there of all places. All I inherited from them was the colour of my skin. It is red in winter when it should go English white. And vampire teeth, which the dentist filed down when I was twelve. Evidently Isaac was a blacksmith and would get blind drunk, charging about the village with his eldest daughter, Fanny, on his shoulders. When she grew up she married a pastor who ran one of those "local missions" so hated by Dickens. He preached fire and brimstone to a naïve poverty-stricken population in Hackney, wringing out the few farthings they possessed with promises of a wonderful life once they were dead and buried. He must have been good at it because sometimes he preached in St. Paul's Cathedral and they made him a Freeman of the City of London.

My grandmother was the pastor's second daughter out of eleven children. The third child, her brother, was reported as "Missing, presumed killed in action" on only his second day out in the trenches. My grandmother was firmly convinced he had deserted to run off to Transylvania, which had always been his childhood dream, using the army as a free ticket as far as Flanders. No one ever heard of him again.

As far as religion was concerned, in the family it died out with my great-grandfather. He preached seven services on Sundays and all his children were obliged to sit in the front row. After the service they were interrogated to make certain they had been listening and God help anyone who gave a wrong answer. No one bothered about the church as soon as he departed to the hereafter.

When it came to adventure my father was worse; volunteering for the RAF the Monday after war was declared, an act which was eventually to cost him his life. He opted for Bomber Command, the unit which had the highest casualty list of the war, seconded only by SOE, the agents sent into occupied Europe. During the period following D-Day 25% of RAF flight crews lost their lives in one month. He died of his war wounds three months before I was born.

My only memory of my grandfather is of an old man lying on the sofa suffering from the bronchitis he contracted in the North Sea, coughing his lungs up while my grandmother fed him bismuth for his stomach ulcers, caused by the prolonged stress of expecting to be blown to pieces from one minute to another. Minesweeping continued until well after the war was over. To think, at the time when I knew him he was younger than I am today.

So much for "King and Country", but in those days, apart from conscripted servicemen who were obliged to engage, military service was the only real opportunity for the working classes to see the world or get out of the routine. My mother had met my step-father in the artillery during the war and they married two years after I was born. They lived together in Dagenham until my mother died in 1989. Albert died one year later. All my family were adventurers at heart.

I inherited this love of adventure. Although Dagenham was always the centre of my world, I first began experimenting at the age of ten. Much to my mother's anguish, one Saturday morning I took a number 25 bus with my pocket money, in the direction of Victoria station. Exactly why remains a mystery to me to this day, but when the bus stopped outside Bow Road underground station a different urge overtook me. I jumped off to explore a tube station on my own for the first time. In the booking hall was a poster advertising a one day unlimited travel ticket, so I immediately bought one. I spent the rest of the day exploring the entire tube network from West Ruislip to

Upminster, passing by Epping and Richmond. My mother was horrified when I returned home with tales of my exploit but it did not end there.

A newspaper, the News Chronicle, edited small booklets in a series called "I-Spy." The objective was for children to go page by page through the booklet discovering various objects, animals, or places, and note the time and day of their observations. There was "I-Spy at the seaside", "I-Spy in the forest", "I-Spy in the train", etc. I bought "I-Spy in London" and, before I was 12, I knew by heart all the London landmarks and monuments, together with a brief history attached to them.

None of my class mates shared my enthusiasm for exploration and in any case I doubt if their parents would have let them wander about. I was fortunate, that's all. One day in Valence public library I stumbled across a book by a guy called Donald Maxwell, entitled *"A Detective in Essex"*. Thumbing through it, I read of his explorations in the country villages of Essex and, having been the official artist in the Royal Navy during the first war, Maxwell's pages were full of sketches of the places he had visited. I stuffed the book into my duffle bag. A treasure like this was far too valuable to be obliged to return to the library after only two weeks.

Maxwell had died in 1936 and this was all old stuff. Fobbing Harbour, where the smugglers who were guided by a beacon in the curious church tower, bringing ashore kegs of spirits and sacks of tobacco to be hidden by the accomplice rector, had been drained after the 1953 flooding of Canvey Island, but the old wooden harbour walls still stood in the fields as witnesses to a bygone age. For me it was like a whack over the head with a stick and my "I-Spy" books immediately gave way to Ordnance Survey maps. As I grew older my topographical explorations expanded from Essex into Kent.

Anyway, in the radio operators' school I had mastered the Morse code in record time and could send and receive at nearly thirty words a minute, which was the standard required of a qualified merchant marine radio operator. All that remained was to perfect the peculiarities, such as the maritime version of the Q-code and the post office telegraphic rules and procedures. Pulling a radio and radar apart followed at its own pace but, forgetting swimming, a second menace began to manifest itself. An advanced warning that something was wrong arose during the secondary subjects which we were learning.

Amongst the lessons in the curriculum was typing, as it was quicker to take down rapid Morse messages on a machine than to write them out by hand; speech therapy, as everyone had to loose their working class accents if they were to be correctly understood over a radio-telephone; and we were also taught to dance. This was an added bonus for those who might find themselves on the liners one day. The officers were expected to entertain the passengers after their spell of duty was over. I had the greatest difficulty co-ordinating my movements about the floor and had just decided that dancing was not my particular thing when it rapidly became painfully obvious that I suffered from chronic seasickness.

My sense of balance was completely upset. There was, and still is, something wrong in my ears. A recent diagnosis found I have a build-up of crystals in the inner ear which prevents the free movement of the liquid which governs the balance. When the room begins to move at a different pace to my eyes one tablet of Tanganil will usually do the trick, but in those days I simply had to put up with it. I tried every single remedy for sea-sickness then known to man, from every pill available on the market, chewing orange peel, a needle in one ear, wearing an onion on a piece of string about my neck, down to carrying a dead cat's tail in my left pocket. I tried to console myself with the fact that Nelson was always seasick after leaving port, but his problem cleared up after a few days whereas mine always got worse. Reluctantly I left the school in order to find a job on dry land.

Probably the most valuable lesson which I had learnt at that school was never to be ashamed of admitting that you do not know something. Be frank and right from the start say, "I don't know." One lecturer started off by telling us the tale of a youngster who was being measured up for his first uniform when the tailor asked on which side he dressed. He hesitated, so the tailor prompted him with, "Left or right?" The girls might not know this one, and evidently there are a lot of lads who do not know it either, but the "side on which you dress" is the side your privates fall in a pair of trousers. Having the alternative of left or right he presumed it was a political conversation and replied, "Right." By far the greatest majority of men's trousers are cut left, so he spent his first two years at sea in a very uncomfortable position.

On a more serious note, he then went on to relate how in one port the maintenance team came aboard a tanker and asked a young deck officer if the tanks had been degassed. This is the procedure where, once the oil has been unloaded, the toxic vapours are evacuated from the tanks; which are then ventilated and replaced with fresh air. He had been ashore since the boat had berthed and, as it was now five days after unloading, he presumed the routine had been followed. The maintenance team went below, resulting in three deaths before the fire team with breathing apparatus could rescue the others. The moral of the story is that you can make a bigger fool of yourself by pretending to know something which you do not than if you admit your ignorance on a subject, and, most important of all, on board a ship there is absolutely no room for the slightest error. Everyone's life depends on your honesty. This story has remained in my mind ever since; and having the courage to admit I did not know something helped me learn some valuable lessons which contributed to the rapid advancement which took me out of my initial inarticulate environment.

In order to earn some cash I took the first job going down at the Youth Employment Centre and the next day found myself in front of the manager, a Mr Dove, of Wallis' supermarket in Little Ilford Lane. Mr Dove was an easy going youngish East Ender and there was a family atmosphere in his shop which gave us all a certain sense of duty towards him. Although the shop hours were from 9 to 6 and the girls arrived just before opening time, the boys were very often present before 8am. On Tuesdays the last one in had the job of cleaning the "Bird's Eye", the deep freeze just inside the front door; then afterwards the latecomer had to wash down the shop front. The task invariably fell upon Malcolm, who always had difficulty in getting out of bed.

The job was sportive because on delivery day we made a human chain where the lorry driver parked down the side street while we passed the merchandise from one to another, with Mr Dove standing at the staff entrance directing the airborne cases left, right, centre, or downstairs, depending to which reserve they were destined. The heaviest were cases of flour, sardines, and cans of animal food. The shop motto was, "All you break, you pay for", which guaranteed none of the glass bottled goods ever fell to the ground; while the biscuits simply sailed through the air above our heads. The hardest task was the sugar deliveries which bordered the work of the West Indian slaves on the old plantations. This small shop consumed a whole semi-articulated lorry load of sugar each week. There's a health message there for someone. On Saturdays the boys all arrived shortly after 6am and nobody complained about our hours, the shop was our life.

The managing director, Francis J Wallis, was a self-made millionaire. Although he was always distant he was a decent enough guy and had started off alone with this one grocery shop. When self-service first appeared he expanded, finally owning a warehouse in Barking and nine supermarkets in the immediate region, with his company quoted on the stock exchange. Wallis drove a Bentley with "FJ 111" on the licence plate. His second in command, Glenn, who had been his first manager at Ilford, drove a similar car, except that Glenn had it in for me because of my hair length. He always crept up behind me, then bellowed, "Cut your hair" into my ear, making me jump out of my skin. Short back and sides were still the order of the day for working class boys, while I copied the Beatles concerning my hair style.

Just under Mary's check-out counter by the window was the warning bell which she pressed if either Wallis or Glenn approached the shop, to let everyone know they had to be on their toes. Whenever it rang my instructions were to hide down in the cellar in a special "priest's-hole" amongst the cases of canned soup, waiting for the all-clear. That shop was my first introduction to the world of work but after only three months it became boring routine. I was far too restless to stay there, even though with Wallis we all had the opportunity to make it to managerial position one day if we were serious enough. Everyone in his shops began as a potential management trainee as from their very first day. I felt really shaken eight years later while living in Normandy when I heard on the BBC that an Essex businessman, Francis Wallis, had crashed his plane somewhere in France and had been killed. He was a sincerely generous guy and did not deserve that.

One day I saw an ad in the Dagenham Post for stock takers with Boots' greatest rival, Timothy White's. I had already heard about this job; it involved travelling the length and breadth of the country, doing the inventory of their several hundred branches, ranging from the tiny one man shop at Woodford to the king-sized department stores at Glasgow, Ipswich, Barking and Canterbury. I immediately applied and was taken on. We worked in teams of four, doing a small shop on Monday and Tuesday, then a larger shop on the remaining three days. For bigger shops several teams would meet up and, for the very large ones, it took several teams working the whole week.

Everything was well organised. At first you began by recording in a ledger while your companion called the name of the articles, the quantity and the price of the diverse goods. You rapidly became an expert at mental arithmetic because, although at the time the monetary system was still in pounds, shillings and pence, you could work out the total sum before your companion had the time to count the following articles. Calculations such as seventeen articles at fourteen shillings and eleven pence ha'penny became second nature. During this time you also learnt how to go systematically through a large building without missing a single item. On several occasions many years later I was relieved to discover that the French police are never taught this technique when it comes to executing a search warrant. Expenses were paid, fares refunded in full, with an allowance of 7/6d a day for meals and 37/6d

(£1.17/6d) a night for bed and breakfast. With B&B in a pub at an average of 16/- and a bag of fish and chips at 1/6d, the excess generously rounded off the pay.

I was happy travelling about the country, visiting towns which I would never have seen during my lifetime if I had remained stuck in a nine to five job, as so many of my class mates found themselves until the inevitable day they married. After that it got worse, they had to do overtime. They were obliged to, that was what was expected of working class children once they had left school. At Lymington, seeing as we had all failed our 11+ exam, we were deemed to be of lower intelligence. Hence the boys were taught woodwork, metalwork and technical drawing in preparation for the day when they went to work in a factory, while the girls did needlework and cooking in preparation for the day when they became mothers breeding a new generation of workers. In other words, it was *"Matthew and Son"* by Cat Stevens made manifest. In my class of forty-eight, only two had mothers who went to work. That was something unheard of in those days.

Towards the middle of June we had to do the shop in Coventry which was beautiful and when I first saw it the architecture took my breath away. It still stands to this day in Trinity Street, next to the church of the Holy Trinity. I do not know if the building is an original Tudor construction or, like the Flemish Weavers' House in Canterbury, a clever copy, but I immediately fell under its charm, with the chimneys reminiscent of Hampton Court and the black wooden beams against the white plaster walls. Once inside the stocktaking was the usual routine, but somehow during my evening explorations of the town something was different.

After my beans on toast I returned to the shop to

contemplate its design, comparing it with all the Tudor buildings I had visited while wandering about in the Essex and Kent countryside; then I mounted the steps beside the shop, taking the direction towards the cathedral. Dabbling in magic was the last of my preoccupations but, meandering around the small streets in the immediate vicinity of the two cathedrals, I felt a new sensation, impossible to pin point.

The cathedrals themselves meant nothing special to me. The old one had been bombed during the war and only the walls remained, while the new building was a modern construction. However, the surrounding streets reminded me of the opening of Dickens' book, *The Mystery of Edwin Drood*. Unlike during my inspections of towns and villages as a youngster, here I was suddenly thrown back in time and was walking amongst the ghosts of the inhabitants of over centuries ago. It did not last long, maybe less than a second or maybe longer, but while it lasted it seemed like a timeless voyage through eternity. A strange serenity invaded my whole body and on returning to the boarding house that night I could not sleep. I felt as if I was under an anaesthetic, remembering every instance of my passage in time. Those two buildings held a secret to be discovered.

The following day we finished the shop and took the train back to London, where the weeks passed by as usual. Just like airports the world over, Timothy White's shops, although their outward appearances were all different, the interiors were all identical; the same layout, the same goods, the same prices, even the shop staff all looked much alike. I found it hard to believe that a job which presented so much variety could become routine in such a short time.

Several weeks after doing Coventry our next store was

37

Canterbury. My first evening passed without incident, but as the week progressed I found myself drawn closer and closer to the cathedral where, by Friday, I spent all my free time. A few more weeks passed and the next shop on the list was York. In this city I realised that it was possible to read a cathedral building like a four dimensional book in time. I had already learnt about the mysterious telluric forces which aligned churches in predefined locations during my excursions following Maxwell's detective work in Essex and Kent, but now I began seriously to study religious architecture. There are more components to a church than in a radar but somehow I managed to learn them all off by heart. Any form of religion never even crossed my mind; for me my curious experience in Coventry was linked to the site, not to any particular cult. The stones in themselves are materialist, it's the manner in which they are placed together which conveys the original thoughts and ideas of the masons who cut and built them; but this would take even harder work if I was to penetrate their secrets. After one particularly boring week away from home I came to the conclusion that my job was now getting in my way and that for some reason or another I needed time and should stay close to London. On arriving back at Timothy White's HQ in Southwark Bridge Road, I handed in my notice.

My first priority was to find a new job, but in those days this was no problem. You could lay in bed until midday, buy the noon edition of one of the London papers, *Evening News*, *Evening Standard*, or *The Star*, look through the three or four pages of ads, make a phone call for an immediate interview, then start work the following day. One ad caught my eye. It read: "Wanted, interviewers for road traffic census. 12 hour day, 6/- per hour." It was followed by a London phone number. Six shillings in those days was a small fortune so I jumped at it.

I was asked to come to an obscure office, I think it was somewhere off the Horseferry Road, which was an annexe of the Ministry of Transport specialising in London traffic. An elderly man gave me a brief interview and explained the job. I accepted and was asked to come to a reunion in the same office at the end of the week. Without knowing it, I had taken my first step towards my strange destiny.

CHAPTER 4

The Silver Sword
(Now the Adam & Eve)

On the Friday morning in question I stood in the gloomy offices lost in the backwaters of SW1 along with about thirty others; all successful applicants for the post of interviewers on a project, which we later discovered, consisted of finding alternative routes for Members of Parliament to make their way to and from the House, thus avoiding unnecessary delay in the heavy traffic of central London. It must have been some kind of top secret establishment because all the windows had been boarded up, even though the door stood wide open for ventilation. The first room consisted of what appeared to be an ordinary nondescript office, while the second room resembled a wartime op's room. In the centre was a table covered with a large scale street map of London which I calculated, after my experience with Ordnance Survey maps, must have been in the region of three inches to the mile; while the walls consisted of nothing but filing cabinets. Finally, at the end of a passageway, we came to a large room with chairs set out in semi-circles like an amphitheatre.

We all took a seat in timid expectation, waiting for the

elderly guy who we had seen when we first applied for the job to explain everything. The census procedure was simple enough. The police would cordon off a lane, into which they would direct half a dozen vehicles selected at random from the passing circulation. When they stopped, six interviewers would leap out and try to take down the answers to a dozen or so questions in a short a time as possible before the vehicles were released and the following six were stopped. That seemed simple enough. The questions consisted of the origin and destination of that particular journey, the time the journey had started, the purpose of the journey, and I have forgotten the rest. At the same time two others would be sitting by the roadside counting the traffic flow, separating the vehicles into predefined categories. After half an hour another team would take over to give our eyes a break. The afternoon was taken up in rehearsals, with half the class being the interviewers while the other half stretched their imagination to give the most ridiculous answers possible. By the end of the day we had all mastered the census technique and were given our first rendezvous: 6am, Monday morning, at a point on the westbound side in The Carriage Road, Hyde Park.

When we arrived, the police, the elderly man, and a youngish guy with sandy hair who I had already noticed back at the office on Friday were setting up the site with cones and road signs which read, "Ministry of Transport. Road Traffic Census. Please Stop If Requested." All that remained for us to do was begin the survey. We set up our camp and everything went exactly as the elderly man had explained back at the office, but it was harder work than we had first thought. Being on our feet was nothing, the painful part was the gymnastics of bending in two to be on the same level as the driver of a bubble car then climbing up the side of a lorry, clinging on with one hand while trying to write down the driver's answers with the other. The white coats which we wore rapidly became dusty and half an hour passed very slowly. Any longer and it would have been impossible to focus on the answer sheet and the lads at the roadside equally lost the picture, risking a miscount. At least it was not raining. On top of that I started going deaf in my left ear.

After the first couple of hours a taxi pulled up and a blustering, to be polite, chubby guy descended, paid the driver and, hastily pulling on his white coat, was greeted like a long lost friend by Sandy, who was running the site with the elderly guy. Someone made a joke out of it saying, "There goes the first two hours of his pay." Someone else said something along the lines that Billy Bunter had been expelled from Greyfriars and had come to work with us. In all there was a general feeling of camaraderie on the site and although it was hard going at times, the work was fun. I had already met many different people during my travels with Timothy White but this was different.

As for the ridiculous answers we had made up during rehearsals, I very soon began to wonder if we had not lacked in imagination. Some people resented the intrusion on their privacy, while others took to joking. One guy explained to me in great detail the argument against the fluoridation of drinking water, which was about to be introduced, and gave me a whole stack of accompanying leaflets. Today I realise he was right, but he did not use the same arguments that I now use myself. I took him for a harmless eccentric because, like so many other people, who at the time and many still are even today, I was duped into thinking it was good for the teeth. Another guy was terrified the results would be published and when it came to the reason for his journey he whispered that he was on his way to see his mistress and could I help him think up a good justification for his presence on that particular road and at the time in question. One hell of a lot of homosexuals offered to buy me a drink after I had finished my day. I could not believe it. To begin with I had never realised so many existed and until then I never realised I had such a success, but less than one year later I was going to turn my appearance to a sinister calculated advantage.

On the second day a couple of the lads were missing and by the end of the week we had been thinned down to about twenty. During the break after our half hour on the road we chatted and the smokers shared their cigarettes, but the predominant topic of the conversations was the recent general election where the Conservative government had been overthrown by Harold Wilson and the Labour party. I had absolutely no interest in politics; I was far too engrossed with my cathedrals and at one point had even considered entering the church, but somehow religion in itself held no more interest for me than politics. At 17 I still had no idea whatsoever what the word mysticism might mean although, in my innocence, I was already half way down the road. I was too young to vote, the age of majority was still 21, but I did have definite views on certain topics and during one pause I expressed, in no uncertain terms, my disillusionment with the entire British political system.

During my last year at Lymington some works had begun on one of the wings down by the boys' cloakroom. The end wall was being demolished and various constructions were being prepared. "Woody" was overflowing with excitement and explained to us that the school was being modernised. The old wooden building in the playground, which dated from before the war and which housed eight classrooms, had reached the end of its life and two new science laboratories with all the latest equipment and indoor toilets were going to be built. It sounded marvellous as far as his dream about Harrow was concerned, but for us we were nearing the end of our life in this school so we only half-listened to his enthusiasm. The very day after I left school, five years of my life were wiped off the slate. One of the very first changes planned by the new Wilson government was the introduction of comprehensive education. Amongst other things Lymington was going to be closed down as a secondary school, tough luck "Woody", and annexed to the South East Essex Technical College; hence the modernisation and the new science labs. The only trouble was that the works had begun under Harry Mac's (Harold Macmillan) government and were continued by "Laughing Boy" Sir Alec Douglas-Home during the "thirteen years of Tory misrule," to use the Labour election slogan. Until Wilson arrived on the scene nobody had even heard of comprehensive education. This was the undeniable proof they were all in it together, that everything which happens today has already been planned at least five years in advance, and that elections were nothing more than a formality to maintain the illusion of democracy. That was pretty strong stuff coming from me in those days but I was furious about the fate of my old school, even if I had wished it would burn to the ground during the time I was a pupil.

Later on during the morning Billy Bunter, or Martin to give him his correct name, took me aside and asked if I'd like to go for a drink with him during our midday break. There was already a rumour going around the site that he was a "woofter" so I was a bit wary, thinking he had fallen under the same charm as the dozens of drivers who kept promising me a drink after work. He seemed harmless enough so I accepted, oblivious to the fact that by taking up his offer I was walking towards the precipice which would decide the entire outcome of the rest of my life.

At a few minutes after twelve o'clock we left the site, which was in the King's Road that day, made our way across Belgrave Square, and eventually entered a mews called Wilton Row. We came to a small pub which had been one of the landmarks during my "I-Spy" expeditions but which I had long forgotten. This was the first time I had been inside because while I was still under age, the drinking limit was eighteen at the time, pubs were off my agenda. I marvelled at the ancient interior which had not changed since the days when the Grenadiers, which was also the name of the pub, had taken their last drinks there before setting off for the Battle of Waterloo.

Martin ordered a Martini, which more or less confirmed his orientation in my mind, while I took a lemonade. We sat on an old wooden bench outside under the hanging garden and as soon as I closed my eyes I could imagine the troops crammed into the tiny pub or milling about in the mews and hear the clatter of horses' hooves in nearby Old Barrack Yard. I was sitting amongst ghosts who were nervously laughing and joking about "Boney." There were youngsters who had never set foot outside their village before the recruiting sergeant had banged the drums in front of their church, let alone been abroad; at the same time they were being encouraged by the old-timers who had served in the West Indies and India.

Martin snapped me out of my dream by telling me he liked what I had said about my old school and how the Tories had begun Wilson's work for him long before he was even elected.

Then he started talking about Waterloo and how our ancestors were heroes who died for our country. He was interesting. He discussed history in a manner which would have been totally impossible for Taff and I began to realise I had been missing out on something in school. I told him about my own ancestors, except for me they were not heroes but cannon fodder, sent to die for a "King and Country" which could not care one way or another if they existed or not, so long as they went to make up the number. He asked me if I ever thought they had been betrayed and I replied I had never thought of it in that way. As far as I was concerned it was normal for the working classes. You were born as a self-multiplying unit of commercial consummation and production and when the time came you went to the front. Notwithstanding the theory of the national or international situation, the destiny of my school was proof enough for me that an election has no importance. Martin simply smiled and, after a sandwich, we made our way back to the King's Road.

The weekend came and went, but during the following week Martin took me aside again and asked what I would be doing on the Thursday evening. I had nothing special in mind so he told me there was a pub in Petty France called the Silver Sword. If I could be there at eight in the evening he would introduce me to "some of the boys and girls." He said he always ordered a small barrel of beer at wholesale price which he sold at less than pub price but where the profits went to "the club." I was mystified and he grinned but my curiosity was too great for me even if I did think I might be putting myself in some kind of potential danger. He told me to ask the barman for the "upper room" and wait for him there and to have a beer while I was waiting. This was too much to resist but he refused to answer any questions so I was impatient for Thursday to arrive.

On the appointed day while we were folding up camp he gave me a wink and said, "Don't forget, eight o'clock." Just before eight I came out of St James' Park tube station and wandered about under the drizzle looking for the Silver Sword. I had been out in the cold all day and now it was a miserable autumn evening so by the time I found the pub the warmth inside was welcome. When I entered, the room was full of civil servants having a late drink before going home. I asked the busy barman for the "upper room." He hardly looked at me and without saying anything, pointed to a door in one corner of the room at the end of the bar.

A dark flight of stairs led me to another door which I opened. I was surprised to find myself in a smoke filled room where about thirty people were drinking and chatting together in small groups. Two detached themselves from the main body and approached me without saying anything, watching me with curiosity as if I had just stepped out of a flying saucer. I told them Martin had asked me to come and that he said I should have a beer in waiting. Always without speaking, one went over to a keg which was on one of the tables, took a pint glass, filled it, then came back and handed it to me. Two more joined them, peering at me as if my presence mystified them; and I was really beginning to feel like a Martian when, to my relief, the door opened and in walked Martin. He came straight up to me, put one arm around my shoulder and shook my hand with the other.

"Welcome to the Greater Britain Movement."

I had no idea what he was talking about but several of the other people in the room joined the group around me then began congratulating me in a similar manner to Martin.

"Hi, I'm Mike"; "Hi, I'm Peter"; "Hi, I'm Audrey"; "Hi, I'm Tony; "Hi, I'm Carol"; and finally, when the welcoming was finished, one girl stood in front of me in total silence. She made me feel uneasy. Without shaking my hand she examined me from head to toe. Then, after a long pause, gazing straight into my eyes, she said, "Diana."

CHAPTER 5

From the Upper Room to Greenwich

I can hardly say as my very first evening at the GBM was a howling success. Apart from the recent election, half of the time I could not understand what everyone was talking about and could not care one way or another either. I wandered about with my beer in my hand and at one point someone even asked me if I was interested in politics. I replied, "Not really", to which they asked me what I was doing in a political club. I could have said it was because I thought it was a drinking club, or at the worst, a club for homosexuals, but I let the matter drop. Apart from political issues, the big question on everybody's lips was if a certain "JT" would be coming that evening. Having no idea who "JT" might be I was indifferent as to his person, but after I had been there for about an hour the door of the dark staircase opened and in came Sandy from the census in the company of a fairly heavily built man who immediately reminded me of Sir Oswald Mosley, the leader of the Blackshirts during the 30's. At least this explained to me why Martin and Sandy were the best of friends at the taxi in Hyde Park although otherwise they did not seem to frequent each other much on the site.

"JT" would have been flattered if he had known what I was thinking about him. Mosley was his idol. At home, or rather at his mother's house, "JT" still lived with his mother until well after the age of 30, he kept a full length mirror where he would stand for hours on end imitating Mosley's every gesture. His clothing was out of date and matched that of a Mosley which I had seen in old photographs where he had led the British fascists on marches through London's East End. After a few minutes I learnt that "JT"'s name was John Tyndall although the name meant nothing to me. All I could see was a life-sized replica of Mosley.

Surprisingly, seeing as he had been a major topic of conversation during the first half of the evening, very few people even acknowledged his presence when he did finally arrive. He was in direct competition with the keg of beer which was rapidly emptying. A few members had even started going downstairs to reappear with glasses of some stronger stuff. He did not go further into the room than a few feet from the door, not even taking off his raincoat, which he did at least unbutton. He stood there talking with Martin, whose second name happened to be Webster, and Sandy, whose real name was Denis Pirie. After about ten minutes the venerable "JT" vanished. I never saw him go and that was the last I ever saw of him in my entire lifetime. When Tyndall had gone Denis Pirie came up to me and we had a brief chat about the census before I went back to trying to mingle with the crowd.

Over the following weeks I thought it a bit strange that the leader of a movement such as the GBM would take what appeared to be so little interest in his party, but in reality Tyndall was not so much of a political party leader. He left all the work up to the others, a shrewd businessman at heart along the lines of my great-grandfather. Instead of torquing money out of an unsuspecting simple minded working class population by promising them beatitude in a paradise beyond the grave, Tyndall's aims were set on fleecing wealthier middle-class pensioners by promising them a wonderful new Greater Britain to be proud of, maybe a few years after they were dead. The GBM was nothing more than a trampoline. On paper he was a newspaper owner and publisher. The party magazine *"Spearhead"* was his private property and members were expected to buy a copy, which gave him a basic minimum wage for the time being. He had his sights set higher than the press. As far as he was concerned he was in exactly the same position as Moses with the Israelites, Mohammed on the Hijra, or Joseph Smith and his Mormons on their way to Salt Lake City; he had received a divine mission and was leading his faithful across a temporary desert, in preparation for the day when he would become the leader of a mighty party, with Mosley as his deity.

The GBM was a certain means of keeping the flock together, waiting for better days to arrive; in other words, waiting for some financial support from a few prosperous benefactors. At this stage, if he was going to find some guardian angels he needed publicity and arranging stunts was the best means to gain the headlines. Such stunts included Martin Webster knocking the recently declared Prime Minister of Kenya, Jomo Kenyatta, to the ground outside the Hilton Hotel in Park Lane while Tyndall hurled abuse through a megaphone, from a safe distance away just in case the bullets started to fly. Webster would have made a marvellous sacrifice for the cause but the result was nothing more than Webster being sentenced to six months in Brixton prison with two months off for good behaviour, while Tyndall was fined £25. I believe the traffic census was Webster's first job on being released, although at the time he claimed he had just received the legacy of a bookshop in Luton after the death of an aunt.

The evening wore on and I was beginning to feel tired when Diana came up to me. She asked if I was having a nice time and I politely said yes while at the same time I was wondering how to eclipse like Tyndall without being seen. From the amount of drink flowing I was thinking the evening might turn a bit nasty and now was the right time to leave. Diana proposed we should meet up again, Saturday if that was alright with me, and have a quiet drink together in a pub which she knew in Greenwich. I knew all the pubs in Greenwich from the days when I was certain I would be going to sea. I had spent so much of my free time in the National Maritime Museum, the Royal Observatory, and on the Cutty Sark which was in dry dock, that Greenwich had become my second home; but I had never been in any of the pubs before. She chose the "Crown" opposite the Christ Church in Trafalgar Road, which I later discovered was within walking distance from where she lived. We agreed on the time and at long last I finally found myself outside in the fresh air of Petty France. I was not feeling too good either. I have never smoked in my life and the air in the upper room had become thicker than a fog. On top of that, when I was on the road with Timothy White's I usually drank milk shakes and this was my first séance in what, after two pints, would have become binge drinking if I had not left in time.

The next day, at the new camp of our traffic census, Webster took me aside again and began explaining the workings of the GBM. We were an up and coming political force in Britain but a traitor called Colin Jordan had appropriated the headquarters in Holland Park, which had divided the movement. We had temporarily regrouped using a club styled system to gain a certain legality and our day of retribution was just around the corner. He spoke as if I had always been a member from the start but whose memory needed refreshing. I vaguely remember reading of Colin Jordan several years previously, firstly when he had organised a camp in the Cotswolds, inviting Nazis the world over to reunite in a similar manner to when Cardinal Wolsey organised the Field of the Cloth of Gold, inviting knights from all over Europe to participate. The press was full of the speculation as to whether or not an American Nazi, George Lincoln Rockwell, would show up. The suspense turned into a daily press saga with the police putting a special watch on all the air and sea ports while, in reality, Rockwell had already entered by the back door through the Republic of Ireland before all the fuss had begun.

The second event which had caught my eye concerning Jordan was his marriage with a certain French woman named Françoise, who happened to be the niece of the fashion king, Christian Dior. Along with David Harris, one of our childhood dreams we shared at school was to marry with a well- endowed woman one day. In my mind's eye I had congratulated Jordan on his catch, then forgotten all about him. My main preoccupations at the time were learning the Morse code while at the same time fighting off seasickness. This particular week was seeing the end of the road traffic census project and we would all be dispersing, but Webster made me promise that I would come to the Silver Sword again the following Thursday and I agreed. I remained silent about my rendezvous with Diana the following day. She had insisted that I keep it a secret between us.

Saturday morning, just before opening time, I was standing on the pavement in Trafalgar Road outside the Crown. A few minutes after the doors had opened Diana showed up and we went in. After all these years I have almost forgotten exactly how Diana looked. She was short, slim, and had long black hair and that is about as far as my memory will go. The last time I saw her, a few years ago, she was still short, except now she is chubby and with short grey hair; an elderly lady living in God's waiting room, Eastbourne. The Crown, on the other hand, I can still see it as if I was standing there now. It was one of those old "spit and sawdust" places which I always imagined my great-grandmother had kept. The family joke was that my grandfather had been born in a pub, the Queen Charlotte, just off the Jamaica Road in Bermondsey near the docks. It was not because his mother had given birth on the floor in one corner of the bar, which so many unfortunate women had done in the late 1880's, but because she was the landlord and lived upstairs. In those days, in the poor quarters of London there was a pub very nearly every hundred yards; very small one-roomed affairs which could just about hold a dozen customers at the most, and the Crown in Greenwich was a vestige of this epoch. It did have a garden at the back, so we ordered our drinks and sat outside on the wrought iron chairs under the autumn sunshine.

Diana recited more or less the same story about the GBM, the traitor Jordan, and the headquarters, as Martin had done; but at the same time she warned me against Webster, who she considered to be no better than Jordan himself, a swindler. She told me I would be better off avoiding him and that she would introduce me to some of the other members who were more reliable. I thanked her and the morning passed chatting away very agreeably with the leaves falling into our beer on the iron table.

We sat there all morning and at closing time I offered to take her to the Maritime Museum. Much to my surprise she accepted. She seemed genuinely interested by my expertly guided tour but appeared to be more concerned with some of my own exploits while I was still at school when I imagined myself to be a master mariner. We sat on a bench in the park, high up on Maze Hill overlooking the river, and I told her how one day, with a few friends, we had made a raft out of oil drums and planks, setting off at sunrise on Saturday morning from Dagenham to float down the Thames on the current to Southend and then take the train back home. After receiving complaints from the pilots, who already had a difficult job bringing the shipping up and down the river from the London docks, trying to avoid us, the river police eventually fished us out at Gravesend, which was probably just as well for us. I later found out the Thames estuary could be one of the most dangerous stretches of water around the coast.

Another exploit consisted of going along to Maldon where we were going to requisition a small boat and sail down the Blackwater to West Mersea; but, unfortunately, the owner spotted us and made us pull it ashore, up to our knees in the mud. Other wilder exploits ranged from plotting to blow up the explosives factory at the far end of Fobbing marsh, which should have let the sea back into the drained harbour, to mimicking the Great Train Robbers who had managed to unload two and a half million pounds from a mail train.

The Fobbing Harbour project very nearly cost me my life. I had intended to provoke a cataclysm in the explosives factory by using a radio controlled home-made rocket. I had been an avid radio enthusiast ever since I began school at Lymington, so that side of the adventure presented no immediate problems for me, but I had no experience concerning ballistics even though I had gained a vile reputation with both my physics and chemistry teachers; notwithstanding I was often top of my class in chemistry. Somehow the blame for everything going wrong in class always fell upon David Harris, who sat next to me, and it was only normal that he had been a participant in the Fobbing project from the beginning.

Together we concocted a "machine infernal" in the form of a canon which we designed and which we built in secret during one Friday afternoon woodwork class. Metalwork class would have been more appropriate but, as we were both hopeless in that art, we never took that into consideration. In Britain, during the month of October, at 4pm, after school, it is already dark; which added a certain furtiveness to our clandestine manoeuvres, especially if there was the usual afternoon fog which rolls in from the Thames. So we took the machine back to my house and set it up in my garden, filling the explosives section with gunpowder which we had extracted from Guy Fawkes Day fireworks. The machine ready, we primed the fuse, "lit the blue touch paper and stood well back," as the printed instructions on all the fireworks of the day stipulated, and waited. There was one God almighty bang which rattled all the windows in the neighbourhood and, after opening our eyes, we saw that our "machine infernal" had vanished off the face of the Earth. It was followed by the most eerie silence imaginable, which lasted for at least a minute, only to be broken by the distant clatter of pieces of our machine landing on some distant roof after a flight into the upper atmosphere. That was the end of the Fobbing Harbour project.

Diana sat there looking at me, nodding to herself, and then she finally said in a very serious voice, "You're crazy, aren't you?" and continued to nod, answering her own question. I could see her mind turning over like a cow chewing the cud and she examined me again in exactly the same manner as on the Thursday evening when we first met. It was very relaxing and peaceful sitting on our bench and as time passed I tried to take her hand but she quickly withdrew it. She immediately apologised and confessed she was homosexual then asked me if I was too. I said, "No," and she replied, "That's funny, you look like one." I thought, "Sod you." And said, "I know, I've just found out the hard way over the past four weeks." She seemed fairly disappointed, lowered her eyes and said, "Do you want to see me again?"

I did not want to lose her; there was some kind of complicity going on between us, although at this stage I could not exactly define our relationship. I told her how Webster had asked me back to the Silver Sword the following Thursday and she promised to be there, suggesting we should arrive before the others, as soon as the pub opened. It sounded like a good idea so I agreed.

I was mystified as to what Diana could see in me, but I felt that for some reason or another she was going to play an important part in my life. There was no way I could have realised she was going to be my second and most important step towards my destiny.

CHAPTER 6

The Greater Britain Movement

Conforming to my very first impression, the Greater Britain Movement was in essence a drinking club. Apart from that, nothing really happened during the six months while I was a member. The Silver Sword was not the only venue on the menu; any pub was a good pretext for the members to hold an improvised reunion. Finally I became so accustomed to the atmosphere of the public house that when I found myself looking for a new job, and having just turned eighteen at the end of October, I decided to give the profession of barman a serious try.

Back at the census, the lads could have been divided into three main categories, all expounding the merits of their own particular trade. They were out of work film extras, out of work sales representatives, and out of work waiters. During my four weeks on the road I had learnt a few tricks of each trade and how to find work in each. For the film industry, the first step was to join "Equity" the show business union and they gave me the addresses of several reliable agencies which specialised in recruiting "atmosphere people", to give the extras their proper title. As far as the salesmen were concerned, they said the best jobs were going in the *Daily Telegraph*. If you were suitable material for selling you would earn the highest pay imaginable, working your product to death, then moving on to richer pastures using the experience which you gained as you went along. Finally, the waiters had given me the address of the "hotel and catering" labour exchange, somewhere in the West End. I called in there and was given the details of a pub called the Bucklersbury Arms, which was looking for a bar/ cellar man. I had no idea as to what the job might involve, but improvising and playing a situation by ear was one of my natural gifts so, clutching my introductory piece of paper, I set off for the City and spent the rest of the afternoon trying to find Budge Row EC4.

It did appear on all the maps which I consulted but it was well hidden. After that I had even greater difficulty in locating Bucklersbury House and, when I did finally stumble upon it by accident, there was no trace of the pub in question, the Bucklersbury Arms. Someone told me it was located in the basement, so I went down to see the guv'nor. The landlord's name was Mr Hole, and I had a hard job keeping a straight face there because only one word kept coming to mind. He seemed to like me and I started on the following Monday. I had no contact with the restaurant staff but the two barmaids were wonderful girls who must have twigged my secret that I had never done the job before and they covered me nicely; but by Friday I hated the job. The Lord Mayor's Show being on the Saturday, I was expected to turn up exceptionally to serve a flux of sightseers. I spent the morning alone sitting in an empty bar. I did learn a lot of things during my week. To begin with, I learnt that I did not know how to make a sandwich properly and that I had no idea how to correctly pack a Schweppes case with empty bottles. You can immediately spot someone who has worked in a pub by giving them some Schweppes bottles to arrange. In all, my week was elucidative but I hated it so much I did not bother to appear the following Monday even though, in record time, I had gained some valuable experience. I prepared myself for a period on the dole, which would give me time to share between my cathedrals and a deepening interest in mysticism which was growing stronger and stronger as each day passed.

The principal activities in the GBM consisted of buying a whole heap of literature from Tyndall's mobile bookshop, which Webster and Pirie invariable carted about with them from place to place, and paper sales, which helped to bolster Tyndall's meagre revenues. A dozen of us would stand in a well-spaced-out line along the edge of the kerb, generally in the Earl's Court Road or Kensington High Street, holding copies of *Spearhead,* trying to catch the attention of the passers-by. On these occasions Diana had a piercing voice and would cry out at the top of her voice, "Read the Spearhead, read a white man's paper, read the Spearhead, only one shilling." Needless to say what my clients appreciated the most in me was the same as at the census and I had almost as many invitations for a drink after the paper sales were over as when I was working this same census. It made Diana laugh.

The other major activity was a singular waste of time. Many street manifestations were planned but never seemed to materialise into anything concrete. The routine was that a "protest" was organized for "X" location at "XX hours" and everyone was expected to show up, on pain of excommunication in the event of unjustified absence. Webster was strict on this point. On arriving at the site the Independent Labour Party would have already installed speakers all along the road, leaving us with no room to manoeuvre. We would stand around for about an hour or so and then Webster would call the meeting off, with all the would-be protesters diving into the nearest pub once the word was given to disperse.

Tyndall never assisted at any of the paper sales and I never saw him once at any of the protest meetings. At the same time he never set foot in the Silver Sword in my presence since my first evening when I was co-opted into membership into the GBM by Webster.

However, all this time Diana was going to work on me as if she was grooming me for a mission which, until then, I had no idea existed. We were seeing each other on a regular basis and several times she took me back to her parents' house in Humber Road in the evening after she had finished work. At other times, when I had been away from London exploring distant cathedrals, churches, museums, and libraries, she would meet me off the train when I came back and we would spend the rest of the evening together. In a very short time her "reliable friends" had totally alienated me from Webster and the executive of the GBM and our conversations took on a new direction.

They began by giving me material which they had obtained from the American Nazi Party in the United States. Having an innate loathing of everything American since a very early age none of this interested me in the slightest, but after a while they introduced me to some of the literature distributed by the traitor Jordan. To say the least, I was curious. The sight of a swastika on his newspapers intrigued me, but I had no more interest in reading the *"National Socialist"* than I had in reading *Spearhead*. Diana suggested that I stopped attending the GBM reunions and the Silver Sword and told me we could work out something interesting between us. Admittedly, after a while the GBM was just as boring as stacking bags of sugar in Wallis' supermarket so I took her up on her offer. During a certain time we did nothing on the political level but simply wandered around London together while I showed her my "I-Spy" circuit, going from landmark to landmark discussing everything imaginable except the GBM.

At home I spent Christmas as usual with my family, but at the start of the New Year I began to have trouble down at the labour exchange. To earn some extra cash I had taken a part time job on the side at a pub which no longer exists, helping out at weekends, being paid in cash after the Sunday midday rush was over. The guv'nor took me on knowing I was a beginner which permitted me to make mistakes while perfecting my knowledge of the trade along with having time free to carry out my own activities, but someone must have denounced me somewhere. My three months on the dole suited me fine but the labour exchange now began threatening to cut me off.

One day, however, Diana was the guide. We took a circle line train to Notting Hill Gate then began walking down Notting Hill towards Holland Park. A few yards past Holland Park station we turned right into Princedale Road and, about half way down, we came across a pub called the Prince of Wales, which we entered.

It was the perfect London pub, bare floorboards, the smell of beer and tobacco, a saloon bar, a public bar, and a back room for intimate conversations. She told me she first started frequenting this place when she was a member of the National Socialist Movement, except she no longer referred to Jordan as the traitor. She gave me the full story of how they had a promising party going until French Jezebel arrived. Jezebel immediately became engaged to Tyndall then, for no apparent reason, threw him over in order to marry his partner Colin Jordan. The more she told me about Jordan and Françoise, the more I became intrigued with this sordid romance based on Nazism. She said Jordan had thrown her out because he was jealous of her. I could not think why such a big Nazi would be jealous of this little girl and presumed that when the fission occurred she had simply backed the losing horse in following Tyndall. We finished our drinks and Diana led me further down the street. All of a sudden she seized my arm, whirling me around to face a shop window and almost pressed my nose against the glass.

"It's Jordan and Françoise," she whispered.

Further along the road a blue Jaguar was parked in front of a shop with heavy shutters. A man was holding one of the doors open and a tall blonde with long hair in an overcoat was standing in the doorway of the shuttered shop. So this was Françoise Dior. I shall remember this scene for the rest of my life and even today I am unable to describe the sensations which ran through my body like an electric shock.

A heavy man, Colin Jordan, appeared behind her. Jordan locked the door of the shop and everyone took a place in the Jaguar, which the third man drove off. Once the Jaguar was out of sight we walked up to what once must have been a shop but which now resembled a citadel. The building itself was crumbling. An iron grill protected a basement area, an armoured door and armoured shutters covered the shop front, while there were two windows up on the first floor covered with chicken wire and another two windows on the second level. Diana kicked the door to see if it had been closed properly then said, "Why don't you join?"

"What, me?"

"You'll be at home here. You see, you'll like it, and you'll meet some interesting people almost as crazy as yourself."

She gave me a fairly accurate description of the interior and we walked back to the Prince of Wales. We were sitting in the back room when all of a sudden she pulled some paper and an envelope out of her handbag and told me to write off for an information pack, to which I duly obeyed. She popped the ready stamped envelope into the pillar box outside Holland Park tube station and I accompanied her as far as Charing Cross then made my own way back home, still puzzled about what she must have had in mind.

About a week or so later my information pack arrived. Inside was a copy of Jordan's newspaper, *"The National Socialist"*, some of the literature which I was already familiar with, and an application form to join the National Socialist Movement. Sitting in a Strand coffee house Diana helped me fill in the form, giving the right answers to all the questions, and again, she was the one who posted the envelope, at Charing Cross station. Another week passed and an invitation arrived asking me to present myself at number 74, Princedale Road, London, W11, at 6pm on the following Friday evening.

The door was opened by the driver of the Jaguar who, after I had introduced myself, welcomed me in much the same manner as Webster had received me on my first evening at the Silver Sword. I sat on a sofa in the reception room then Françoise appeared. I am still unable to describe my first impressions but she handed me a membership card with my photograph inside. I was now a fully paid up member of the British National Socialist Movement, number M 627. The third step towards my destiny had been accomplished.

CHAPTER 7

The National Socialist Movement (I)

In the reception room was a sofa, some armchairs, a boarded up chimney and a door leading to a bookshop which was behind the armoured shutters in front of the building. In one corner was a red swastika flag, on the table was a photograph of Adolf Hitler and, above the chimney, was a notice board underneath the Nazi spread eagle.

To my generation, in 1965, the swastika represented excitement and adventure more than anything else. We had been born after the war and had not experienced the air raids. For me an air raid shelter represented the family story of how, when they were distributed, my grandparents left theirs to rust in one corner of the garden. Half way through their Sunday lunch on the 3rd September, when the wireless announced a state of war existed between Britain and Germany, everyone dropped their knives and forks and ran out into the garden, where they began digging like rabbits to get the shelter installed before the first wave of bombers arrived that afternoon; only to find that most of the nuts and bolts had gone missing. They kept our shelter together with string, waiting for the ironmonger to open the following day. The first of only two major events at Morley Road was when the dog was run over by a tank one night. The Romford Road was closed with tank traps at the Whalebone Lane crossroads so the tanks had to make a detour along Mill Lane as a deviation. When I was born I was named in his honour; our canine member of the family who became a war hero, Terry. The second was one night when my mother came home on leave during an air raid. She never bothered to sleep in the shelter and when she slipped into bed, in the dark as the blackout prevented her from undressing with a light on, she found herself between the sheets next to a lump of red hot shrapnel. Next day she discovered a hole in the ceiling where it had fallen through the roof and onto her bed. A few minutes earlier and it would have killed her. During the war she had several close escapes which never seemed to bother her. The event which persuaded her to join the army was one midday while she was working in Plessey's aircraft components factory in Romford. She was on her way to buy her fish and chips when a Messerschmitt flew down South Street, machine gunning the workers on their way out for lunch. She was so angry about the effrontery of the Germans that instead of returning to the factory she entered the army recruiting agency, which was only a few yards further down the road from the chip shop. She bought a packet of cigarettes with her "King's shilling." Following this incident the factory was transferred to a tunnel of the present day Central Line underground railway between Newbury Park and Leytonstone stations which had recently been dug and was not yet operational. The 5 mile long underground factory was serviced by a small electric train.

Twenty years after the war had ended the films and television were still portraying the achievements of our troops and the allies giving the illusion the war was one great experience of exploits and patriotism which my generation was unfortunate to have missed. In joining the NSM I had the impression I would be partaking in something, "extreme" to say the least, except by wearing the swastika I was taking sides with Guy Fawkes.

Post-war Eastern Europe had been occupied by the Soviets and the Iron Curtain had the backfire effect of retarding history during the forty-five years during which Moscow ruled over the workers' paradise. All western scientific expeditions into Soviet-held territories were forbidden. It has only been recently that Professor Ballard has been able to explore in full the depths of Black Sea, where the waterline of the original fresh water lake was 100 metres below its present level, revealing traces of the villages of the inhabitants who lived at the time of Noah's flood, when the Mediterranean burst through the Bosphorus. Mount Ararat was equally under Soviet control and out of bounds. At the same time the extermination camps were all in Soviet held territory and all access met with the same refusal as the archaeological sites elsewhere. It has only been with the end of the Iron Curtain the full truth, which until then was vague, has begun to be revealed. It is more than probable that if the Holocaust had been presented in 1965, in the same way as it is today and the camps accessible, the entire future of National Socialism would have been different. As it was, "War in the Air" and similar televised episodes of life during the war insisted only on the heroic aspects of this changing point in history.

My only memory of this first evening at Princedale Road is of a few youngsters arriving and pinning some newspaper clippings onto the notice board, which had something to do with a fire somewhere but I did not bother to read. They seemed very excited about the articles but, being new, I was totally out of place. I would only settle in during the weeks which followed, once I had begun to get to know everyone.

Life at Princedale Road was divided between Friday evenings and Saturday afternoons. Friday evening was Françoise's occupation, organising secretarial work, ranging from counting leaflets and stickers into bundles of twenty-five, preparing the mail for distant members and typing. Saturday afternoon was Jordan's domain and involved outside activities, such as paper sales down at Notting Hill High Street and protest marches along a deserted Whitehall. At first I belonged to the Friday activists and was far from being at ease. They might not have been homosexuals but they were certainly very boyish. I noticed that Françoise seemed to have a strange relationship with these lads and, what worried me, she began counting me in amongst them. There were the two newspaper clippers named Thorne and Evans, plus three or four others. In general I had the impression my presence in the Friday club was not very welcome by the other members. The press clippings were of a fire which had destroyed the synagogue at Brondesbury. I had taken no notice at the time and in any case the clippings were gone the following week. I quickly placed myself in the Saturday group, which could be further divided into two distinct sub-groups: namely upright healthy solid Nazis and Nazis who preferred to tank up in the Prince of Wales before consecrating the rest of their afternoon to the cause. After an apprenticeship in the GBM I obviously went to make up part of the latter.

The cause for which Jordan crusaded was to "Stop the Coloured Invasion." It was not that any of us, except a small hard core, had anything personal against the blacks, but the recently independent Jamaica was progressively being bankrupted by the International Monetary Fund and the former Conservative Minister of Transport, Ernest Marples, had encouraged a massive immigration of West Indian workers to man the London Transport system during the British labour shortages. It did not stop there and in the short lapse of time since the days of my childhood, when we would run behind the coal cart calling out "nigger" to the black faced coalies hoping they would chase us, West Indians were becoming more and more an everyday part of the British scene. At the time anyone with a grain of sense could have predicted Harold Wilson's "Great Leap Forward" would be the thin end of the wedge, eventually leading to the economic crisis we have today and, according to Jordan's policies, the immigrants were to blame.

Françoise, on the other hand, had her own ideas. Outwardly she hated Jews to the core, but in reality her anti-Semitism was a strictly personal affair which no one could have perceived through simple observation. Later I discovered that inwardly she was firmly convinced Christian Dior had died as the result of a Jewish plot. Her reasoning was far more complex but to the press she was nothing more than a fanatical Nazi who had found her ideal in a British Nazi movement. Being in the Saturday group I saw very little of her. Our leader was a certain Hugh Hughes, an ex-guardsman who had been discharged after an incident where "thunderflashes" were thrown during an election meeting, while his deputy was Malcolm Sparks, the same age as me and who lived in Woodford Green. I visited Spark's house several times. He seemed almost as crazy as me, with his plans for "Operation WC," an idea to plant some plastic explosives on the crotch of Winston Churchill's statue on the green and blast it to atoms, at the same time spreading Nazi literature about the immediate vicinity. Like everyone else he knew I had previously been a member of the GBM, except he was less convinced that I had broken all ties with them and thought I was acting as some kind of a spy for Tyndall, so he left me out of all his other plans. Venerating the SS, he also disapproved of the Prince of Wales crew holding their own private reunions in the back room before activities began. All the same, he had a certain instinct but was unable to divine my only contact from my past days was with Diana, who kept pestering me for news about Françoise and Jordan.

At the same time as my activities with the NSM, I was entering deeper and deeper into a world of mysticism and magic, up to the point where a few simple experiments which could be performed by anyone finally convinced me the ancestors knew some sort of lost secrets when they built their cathedrals. I could find nothing particularly new in London so I decided to return to the site of my first voyage in time. I wrote off for a job as barman in the Coventry four stars international, the Hotel Leofric, and to my surprise by return of post received an invitation for an interview. Not having much cash to spare I set out at 4am and thumbed a lift to the City of Three Spires. The sub-manager showed me all over the hotel, it was enormous compared with those I had seen while on the road with Timothy White, and he explained the job. If I accepted I would work in the main cellar during the day and give a hand in any one of the bars in the evening if there was a heavy workload. There were five bars, two restaurants, and a ballroom attached to the hotel and the manager assured me I would be kept busy. The job was mine if I wanted it. I took it.

The main cellar was just inside the staff entrance at the back of the hotel at basement level and was kept continually locked even while Martin the cellarman and I were working inside. The first thing I had to do was to learn the names and corresponding number in the list of over five hundred different wines and to be able to find them at an internal phone call's notice. The cellar was so gigantic there was room for all the bottles in racks around the walls, a warm room for the reds, barrels against the far wall feeding the beer pumps upstairs, and space for the day to day workings of a bar cellar. For those who "lived-in" there was a large house just off the city centre where I shared a room with Martin, my work companion. He was an ex-public schoolboy, along with most of the other employees in the restaurants and kitchen. The Leofric was a training hotel for future hotel managers and the brewery recruited in the upper schools. The only trouble was, and probably still is, public school is synonymous with homosexuality.

With a few drinks after work everyone let their hair down. My working day was the usual pub hours so I had my afternoons off to return to the cathedrals but quickly decided I was getting nowhere in mysticism. Coventry had simply been an introduction to another world, without going any farther. At the Leofric I set about learning as much as possible from the public school system. If it was at the Bucklersbury Arms I discovered I was unable to make a sandwich properly, it was here I realised I was uneducated enough not to know how to eat long spaghetti correctly by rolling it in my spoon with a fork. Until then the only spaghetti I had seen in my life was the canned Heinz variety. Amongst other things, I also learnt how to spell "aperitif" correctly. I used to chat with one guy in the kitchen until one day Martin told me he was a commis. This is the French technical term for a debutant chef but I, in my ignorance, interpreted it as a "commie," a communist, so I avoided the poor fellow for the rest of my stay at the hotel.

The regular clients in the bars taught me a lot. Amongst them was Father David, an unbelievably rich catholic priest, who would settle down in the lounge at the start of the evening and drink half a bottle of Martell Cordon Bleu cognac before returning to his flock. In two months he taught me the entire catholic dogma. I absorbed every grain of information possible from the international clients and began copying their mannerisms, but one experience obliquely helped change my destiny. One frequent visitor to the ballroom bar was Charles Forte, later to become Baron Forte. For some reason or another we got on together like a house on fire and chatted at the end of the bar for ages on end while my boss could only grind his teeth, having to do all the work himself. Forte even offered me a job if I wanted but remembering the slaves working at his sandwich bar in the Strand, I politely declined. Maybe he had something better in mind but after my failure with Coventry cathedral I had decided to return to London. I missed Forte but most of all, I missed his mistress. She never spoke a word, but to this day I can honestly say she was the most beautiful woman I have ever met in my entire life. She never said anything for the simple reason she could not, she was French and spoke no English. After only two months in the Leofric I did return, a thousand times wiser and much enlightened, to London; but at the same time I was now determined that one day I would eventually marry a French girl.

CHAPTER 8

The National Socialist Movement (II)

Back in London the first thing to do, as usual, was to find a job. I went down to the dingy building in the Southwark Bridge Road and called in to see my former boss Peter Salmon at Timothy White's. I asked if I could have my old job back. It was against company policy but reluctantly he agreed. To be closer to Princedale Road I found an apartment in Campden Hill, but back in HQ things had changed.

Thorne, Evans, and their companions had all emigrated to Australia and membership had thinned down drastically. I remembered very little about them and in their absence had difficulty to recall exactly who they were. The leader of their group appeared to have been David Thorne who was about a year or so older than myself. Another member of the Friday club had been Michael Trowbridge, a fairly heavily built guy who was always dressed in a dirty raincoat and never seemed to have anything to say. In a similar silence stood "the undertaker," or John Evans, who spoke even less than the others, if at all. He earned his title from the fact that he drove a hearse, professionally or by fantasy I have no idea but he looked the part. Considering the secret which they shared I now understand their silence; after burning a synagogue I doubt if anyone would have much to say conversationally in a similar situation. Raymond Hemsworth was different, and on the rare occasions when we found ourselves together we had chatted mostly about my work. He wanted to become a dispensing chemist and, when he discovered I had once worked for Timothy White's, he wanted to know all about the firm. The Friday club had now vanished into thin air but I did not miss their absence.

The first thing Jordan said on my return was something about my being three months in retard with my subscriptions, so I paid up. At the same time I had a brilliant idea and stocked up with an abnormal quantity of stickers and posters. My job travelling the country at Timothy White's expense was the perfect vehicle for spreading the word as far afield as possible; and very soon swastikas were appearing in the most unlikely locations, ranging from Lands End and Weston Super Mare, to Glasgow and Blackpool. As I later found out from Scotland Yard, to the frustration of Special Branch the entire country was being covered with Nazi literature and nobody knew how, not even Jordan himself.

There were also fewer and fewer members of the Prince of Wales crew present and as the autumn wore on visits from Hughes, Sparks, and their followers likewise gradually ceased. Exactly as with Thorn and Evans, they had the same reasons to avoid HQ and in the end even Jordan himself vanished. Before he went he gave me a strange task to accomplish. At the rear of the *Daily Express* building in Fleet Street was the staff entrance. Just inside was a flight of stairs which eventually led to the top floor where there was a balcony. My job was to throw a bag full of leaflets over the Lord Mayor's parade which would pass below.

When I arrived at the balcony it was crowded with journalists and typists waiting for the parade so I abandoned the *Express*. Back in the street I scoured the area looking for a similar building on the Lord Mayor's route and eventually discovered the front door of Unilever House was open and the building deserted. I took a lift to the top floor and made my way up to the roof. In due time the procession passed below and I threw my leaflets over the edge but the wind was in the wrong direction. Instead of falling, a gust lifted them skyward and they all blew back towards me over the roof. At least I had tried. Jordan thanked me for the effort then drove off to Coventry.

Françoise was left alone. I continued to spread the word up and down the country except when I was not away with my job and worked in or near London I took Françoise along with me. Instead of Jordan and Tyndall's publicity stunts this might not have been the kind of headstrong life she had expected in the NSM but it was sensational; taking the last tube train from Holland Park, painting and pasting in different locations, then taking the taxi ride back to Princedale Road. After a while I gave her a hand cooking some simple meals which we ate together down in the basement kitchen. One evening before calling in I picked a few of the remaining frost bitten flowers in Avondale Park at the end of Princedale Road and made a small bouquet. When I gave it to her she cried; it was the first time since she had set foot in Britain that someone had given her some flowers.

As the Christmas holidays approached stocktaking became useless, so us stock takers were farmed out to work in various shops here and there where an extra hand might be needed. I was counting on going to the Notting Hill branch but instead was sent to Hornchurch, closer to my parents which made visits to HQ impossible. I never realised Françoise was going to be alone throughout the holidays otherwise I would have arranged something. As it was, when I showed up just after New Year she could hardly contain her joy. After that we went out very nearly every night until one evening in January we were walking towards Notting Hill when I saw one of my posters which I had put up several evenings beforehand laying on the ground. It had been raining heavily during the day so it must have fallen off. I had just picked it up to give it some extra paste when a car drew up; three policemen jumped out and arrested me. I spent the night in the cells at Notting Hill nick and was going desperate to get out. Bail was refused.

Next morning I asked the sergeant who had arrested me to call my boss in Southwark Bridge Road to ask him to send my pay check and cards to HQ. The poor guy was shattered; their objective in arresting me was simply to give me a lesson as a deterrent. I explained I was claiming expenses for being in a place where I was not and all I could expect was the sack. Later on, during the morning at Marylebone court, I was fined the maximum of £2 for fly posting. In court I must have given everyone the impression I was really hard up because whenever I went out on activities at night I never carried anything in my pockets which I might lose, including money, so although the fine was a negligible sum the sergeant advised me to ask for five days in which to pay otherwise I would be kept in until the fine was settled. I said it was humiliating and he told me how once he overlooked a penny in one of his prisoner's pockets during a search and when the detainee arrived in prison the remainder of his sentence was one hell on earth. During a more thorough search at Brixton the clerk recorded, "Prisoner's possessions, one penny." The other inmates never let him forget it with jokes such as, "Didn't you know the loos are free in here." Courts, including the prisoners' waiting room can be great places for jokes. The five days delay gave me time to go home, collect my cash, and then return to pay the gaoler at the court. That episode also spelt the end of my apartment in Campden Hill which I reluctantly renounced. When I finally arrived at HQ Françoise hugged me and said I could live there with her for the time being if I wished, so I moved in.

Instead of frightening me off, the police had succeeded in making me a full time Nazi. This was my fourth step towards my destiny.

CHAPTER 9

Getting to know Françoise Dior

Françoise was obsessed with homosexuals; hence the string of girly-boys who had made up her Friday secretarial sessions, and she was firmly convinced I was one of them. This originated with her love for her uncle Christian, a 100% homosexual, who had replaced her father in her life; and, not wishing to disappoint her, I said neither yes nor no, letting her believe whichever fantasy pleased her. After my introductory experience at the census followed by my two months initiation at the Leofric I could certainly play the part to perfection.

At my own suggestion she accepted me as her private secretary. I was not expected to work for nothing. She said she could only afford to pay me £2,10/- a week. The dole was £3,7/6 but one of the members I had met before leaving for Coventry was a flunky at Buckingham Palace who told me the pay in his job was thirty shillings. As he put it, the figure was negligible when you had the honour of serving the Queen in person. Coming from a Nazi I always thought this was sick stuff and when I explained to Françoise that by working for the Nazi queen of Britain I would be very well paid in comparison, she laughed. This was the first time I had seen her laugh since joining the movement. The pay was poor because, contrary to an illusion completely fabricated by the press and refuelled by people who have never met her, Françoise was always flat broke from one day to another. We lived for most of the time on the reserve I had accumulated while serving in the bars at the Leofric and the excess of my expenses with Timothy White's.

As time passed our nocturnal activities increased, but during the daytime I took her out on my "I-Spy" guided tours of London. She loved it and said since she had lived in Britain she had never visited one single monument. While I had been away in Coventry, Françoise had bought an Alsatian dog for company which she called Helga. This dog was to eventually become a determining factor in our lives but, in the meantime, taking the dog for a walk was an excellent pretext to be wandering about late at night putting up posters.

One thing I discovered was that during the infrequent visits Jordan made to HQ, and which never lasted more than a couple of days at the most, they were continually quarrelling. When he was not in front of the press Jordan seemed totally incapable of expressing himself coherently. For a Cambridge university graduate he continually fell back on his working class origins, with his broken speech interspersed with fuck this, and fuck that, while at times, when he lost control of himself, fuck was used at every second word he uttered. Finally, believing she was dealing with a sincere homosexual, Françoise confessed to me her disillusionment with Jordan and explained exactly how she had arrived in Britain.

Her first husband had been Robert-Henri de Caumont la Force, a count from a ducal family in France and she had been the queen of Paris. She did not go into detail about her divorce but said she had adopted Nazism just before her separation and had begun to form a following in France, which I later found out was not exactly true. When she read about the British Nazis in the press she was determined to marry the leader of these British Nazis, "whoever he might be" to use her exact words. On arrival she found two of them, Tyndall and Jordan, so she had an alternative. She chose Tyndall because he had a certain refinement, whereas Jordan was the epitome of vulgarity. The unsuspecting Tyndall immediately fell into her honey trap so she took him on holiday in Paris and the Black Forest. She could hardly believe her bad luck; Tyndall remained impotent all the time, simply lying there in bed without even trying anything.

She was just beginning to despair when both Tyndall and Jordan, along with several other members including Denis Pirie, were arrested on public order charges and sent to prison. One day, she was entering Britain when the immigration officer stopped her and took her into a back room. Britain, not being a member of the European Union at the time, meant that Françoise was an alien like any other French national with the exception: she was an undesirable alien. On the order sheet she was to be refused entry. They were about to send her back to France when she protested, saying she was in the process of being married with a British citizen. The immigration officer, half believing her, gave her an entry visa for three weeks, the time required to publish the banns and accomplish the feat.

The only trouble was that Tyndall, her fiancé, was still inside while Jordan had recently been released. Taking second best, Françoise arranged their marriage in a quicker time than she had become engaged to Tyndall. Not taking the risk of leaving Britain and being rejected again, this time permanently, she became engaged to Jordan on the spot. The fable about them becoming engaged up in the air between London and Paris originated with Françoise herself. During a press interview she told the journalist that Jordan had proposed to her, which puts the blame for her defection from Tyndall squarely on Jordan's shoulders, in an aircraft bound for Paris, while at the same time she avoids any explanation as to what she might be doing heading for France in Jordan's company while still officially betrothed to Tyndall. The first thing she did after their marriage was to apply for, and obtain, British nationality which she kept for the rest of her life.

Less than one week after the marriage Françoise realised she had jumped out of the frying pan into the fire. If Tyndall was impotent, Jordan actually took his mother along with them on their honeymoon in a croft which he squatted in the Highlands. On top of that, Jordan, the same as Tyndall, lived with his mother even though he was 40 at the time. She was dealing with two Führers who were, in reality, mummy's boys.

Jordan's mother hated her from the very start for trying to take her baby away from her. Françoise always slept, as is the French custom, in the total dark, while at the Jordans' home everyone had English style thin curtains which let in the light as soon as the sun rose. Jordan's mother refused any modification to the windows, while Jordan sided with his mother in the ensuing argument; with the result that Françoise took to sleeping on a mattress in a cupboard under the stairs.

The other result of this marriage was the schism of the British Nazi movement. When Tyndall saw the press reports he cried his eyes out for over a week in his cell. He had kept his copy of the keys to Princedale Road so, in retaliation, on his release he rallied the strong arm of his faithful; then, during the night of one of Jordan's prolonged absences from London, he emptied HQ of all the equipment and files. Jordan tried to take action in justice but he had overlooked one small detail. He had forgotten to expel the dissidents from the movement; so the judge passed the reasonable decision of seeing as all persons concerned were members of the same organisation, no theft had occurred. The Greater Britain Movement had been born.

At a later date, Tyndall was to burst into tears again. He had invited a few of his faithful to his birthday party which he held at his mother's house. It was a typical south London suburban terraced house with front and back parlours. The faithful were all sitting in the front room listening to one of Tyndall's Mosley inspired speeches with all the Mosley inspired gestures and trappings when his mother brought in the birthday cake, covered with many candles, and set it on the table. He blew out the candles amongst much cheering and hand clapping; and was just about to slice off the portions when, all of a sudden, someone came in from the back room where the television had been switched on. The refractory said, "It's time for Ready, Steady, Go!" This was a pop show screened every Friday evening with musicians who mimed to their latest records and was presented by a local girl, Cathy McGowan from Streatham. Everyone dashed out to the back parlour, leaving Tyndall alone, crying over his mother's abandoned birthday cake.

When Françoise had ended her confession I suddenly remembered Diana, who I had totally forgotten since my departure for Coventry. On hearing I had been one of Diana's acolytes Françoise then made a second confession: she was homosexual herself, or rather bi. She told me how she had been initiated into the Sapphic art at the age of eight by the nanny who her mother had engaged to look after her as a child. During the short absence of her fiancés she had taken Diana's virginity. Now I understood everything. Had I been more experienced beforehand, and in view of the fact that I knew of Diana's homosexuality, I would have understood her infatuation with Françoise as from the beginning but, at 18, I had missed it all. Her plan was, to be exact, by making me her slave and by planting me into the NSM, Diana had counted on using me as her passport back to Françoise. She had chosen the perfect candidate for her plot as from the moment she first set eyes on me at the Silver Sword. Although I had grown very fond of her, she was now best forgotten. It would be another forty-three years before I was to see her again, long after she had settled down in Eastbourne in order to be nearer Tyndall and Pirie's retirement dwellings in Brighton and Hove district.

The winter was growing colder and colder every day and HQ began to resemble a deep freeze. Françoise's personal fortune, if you could call it that, had nothing to do with the fashion house of her uncle. The central part of her "Jewish plot" was that some Jewish conspirators had killed Christian and had appropriated his fortune and fashion house, but with the passage of time I eventually arrived at the truth of the affair. The little money which Françoise had at her disposition originated with her maternal grandfather. He had been the architect who had built the square de l' Opéra, the rue Caumartin and adjoining streets in Paris, some property in the Basque town of St Jean de Luz, along with the seafront at Tangiers which he had sold believing it would make a loss, and, finally, the cathedral and governor's palace in the west African colony of Dakar. On his death, under complicated French inheritance law, her mother benefited of the greater part of his fortune with his widow, the spouse being only fifth on the French legal list, inheriting only a minimal donator's part.

On the grandmother's death Françoise was only second in line after her mother, inheriting nothing directly from her grandfather. She simply acquired the *"part reservatrice"* (French legal technical term with no English equivalent), of the part of her grandfather's fortune which he had left to his wife. In other words Françoise indirectly received a negligible portion of the original estate of her grandfather.

It was already a rock bottom figure which had been rapidly depleted even before she had left France to begin her Nazi career in Britain. The little which remained after her engagement with Tyndall was immediately snapped up by Jordan as "funds for the cause." On top of that he was greedy and demanded a monthly revenue if she was to remain in London. His infrequent visits to HQ were nothing more than to collect his Danegeld. During their quarrels Jordan continually insisted that he would leave Françoise the entire British Nazi movement on the condition they made mutual wills. There was something sinister in this agreement as from the start. He was already nine years her senior and statistically women live longer than their husbands. This would have been fine from Jordan's point of view; he had nothing to lose.

The building at Princedale Road was the property of Arnold Leese's widow. Captain Leese was a first war veterinary surgeon who had made his fortune with a renowned medical text book on treating camels which he had started writing while he was in military service in the east. He was one of the original "animals' rights" crusaders and had something personal against Kashrut, or kosher slaughter, which rapidly degenerated into anti-Semitism in general. Speaking from my professional experience which I later acquired in Normandy and without going into boring detail, if he had really witnessed and had understood kosher slaughter, as I personally did during my five years while working in the French veterinary service many years after my first arrival in France, he would have realised that Kashrut was probably the most humane slaughter possible, even compared with modern European stunning methods. His living in the east I can only presume he must have confused it with the ghastly Halal slaughter which, although presented to the public as similar to kosher slaughter, is two worlds apart. This is only my personal opinion based on first-hand experience as a veterinary technician.

Nevertheless, on his return to Britain, Leese joined the British Fascists, later founding his own movement, the Imperial Fascists, resurrecting the forgotten myth of Jewish ritual murder which had gained ground during the Middle Ages when people believed in witches and the Devil, and when you could be burnt at the stake for believing the earth was round. Unbelievably, and taking things even further, he was the very first person to advocate the mass murder of Jews by means of gas chambers, as early as 1935!

His widow gave Jordan unlimited use of the building at Princedale Road in sentimental memory of her husband. Jordan evidently knew absolutely nothing of French inheritance law because, by having a daughter by her first marriage, Françoise's girl child would have been first in line after her death; while her mother, if she might have still been alive at the death, would have been second in line, so any will made by Françoise would have been of extremely little value. (As a point of interest, any brothers or sisters came third, with their children, the nieces and nephews, in fourth place leaving the spouse only fifth in line). All the same, he never gave up and insisted on the mutual wills on every visit.

As for Françoise inheriting the NSM, it was now worthless.

Far from their living in Australia, the Stoke Newington police had arrested the Friday club along with the members of the Saturday club who had gone to make up a second group of synagogue arsonists with the result that membership of the NSM had dropped to zero overnight. As far as I knew I was the only remaining member.

By the time I went to live in HQ she was already worse than flat broke and, as the winter progressed, the building became so cold she would remain in her dressing gown throughout the mornings and sit in the basement kitchen, light the gas oven and sit with her feet inside to keep warm. Half way down the road was a Greek grocer and we would buy our supplies there on credit, waiting for her monthly income to arrive from Paris. Her only real expenditure was her visits to the Jewish hairdresser in Notting Hill. As far as she was concerned it was too bad for the ideology, Maurice Stein was the best coiffeur in the west of London and he treated her as a prize client. It was then I discovered her natural colour was brunette and years of dying had completely ruined and discoloured her hair.

At night we would be out with our stickers and posters. One day she was politely invited to Stoke Newington police station for questioning, (the expression "wanted for questioning" does not exist in English law although the police use many unimaginable ploys to give the impression), and to make a statement concerning the synagogue arsons, which was equally not obligatory. At this point nothing came of it. While she was being interviewed one of the officers asked me, off the record, what I thought of everything myself. The Friday evening club had burnt their synagogue before I had become a member of the NSM and the Saturday afternoon club had burnt theirs while I was living in Coventry, so I considered myself well out of it all. The trial of Hughes began at the Old Bailey so we had the added excitement of painting swastikas and slogans on the gates and walls of Brixton prison where he was incarcerated which caused quite a stir. After our initial success in the press we decided to paint the Old Bailey which, to the embarrassment of poor Hughes, caused an even greater stir. Françoise was beginning to come alive again but her revival was short lived.

One night we were awakened by a great crashing sound which shook the entire building and I thought we were under attack. Outside I discovered a chunk of the cement balustrade on the upper floor had detached itself and had fallen to the pavement. The whole slum was slowly crumbling. Then we were invaded by rats. I never saw any but could hear their distinctive clicking sound as they ran through the spaces between the floorboards and the ceilings below.

At the same time Françoise had developed an extremely bad cold; and in the evening she sat wrapped in a blanket with her feet in the oven, sobbing softly to herself. I went down to the Boots all night chemist at Aldgate for some medicines, which I could obtain without a prescription by using my Timothy White's staff card which I had kept after getting the push, then mixed her up some hot Ribena and comforted her. *Inutile* to say, we spent the night in bed together. I had just turned nineteen and Françoise was approaching her thirty-fourth birthday. The fifth step towards my destiny was accomplished.

CHAPTER 10

A Tale of Three Cities: London, Paris and Nice

Françoise never completely recovered from her bad cold and as the days passed I never even suggested going out on activities at night. Jordan came and went to collect his Danegeld from Françoise but this did not worry me, they slept in rooms apart. He was on floor one while she was on floor two and their continual quarrel about heritage and mutual wills took place in the basement kitchen. Finally, in the deepest shock, I understood she had abandoned life and was letting herself slowly die; but what could I do? Remembering her tales of her former life in Paris there was only one thing possible, she must return to France as soon as possible, otherwise it would be too late.

With unbelievable difficulty I eventually managed to persuade her we could be far more useful to the cause, what cause, in France, and so, during the day of Monday, 14th March she packed her bags ready to leave London and her "Führer in carpet slippers" behind her once and for all. We took the suburban train from Liverpool Street to Chadwell Heath where I packed my own bags at my parents' home and, after having a marvellous last meal with my mother in the Pakistani restaurant in Ilford, we spent the night in a hotel in Romford. The following day we said goodbye to my parents, then deposited our suitcases in two left luggage lockers at Victoria station before buying a one way sleeping berth ticket to Paris on the "Night Ferry" train to Paris.

The Stoke Newington police were later to present our departure as evidence that Françoise had fled the country in connection with the synagogue arsons. As no justification for this presumption was ever offered in court, their assertion was of no value. As far as she was concerned she had replied to their invitation and had subsequently made a statement. There had never been any question of her being recalled to Stoke Newington a second time. We had left Britain through the regular channels so there was no suggestion that we tried to mask our departure. Everything was in order.

The day passed worse than slowly. We took a midday meal in an Italian restaurant in Kensington High Street, then bought some perfume and cosmetics, which are cheaper in Britain than in France. We then visited the hairdresser in the Army & Navy Stores at Victoria where we spruced ourselves up before changing our lifestyle. As the evening wore on we took our last drinks in London in the Duke of Boots (Wellington) pub in Eaton Terrace and, after what seemed an eternal wait, it was time to board our train. We passed immigration control in the customs shed at Victoria, where the immigration officer treated Françoise as if she was royalty. Although she was now simply Mrs Jordan of British nationality her only travel document was her French passport, in the name of Madame the Countess of Caumont la Force.

We sought out our cabin, closed the blinds and settled

into our bedroom for the night. We did not get much sleep in, or at least, I did not. On the trip down to the coast we were up for most of the time, drinking beer and chatting with the carriage steward, who had taken an immediate liking to the dog Helga. He was one of the old timers who had the privilege of frequenting most of the European aristocracy during his service in the better days of the past. Françoise was one more countess amongst the hundreds he had attended during his long career on the international *"Wagons-Lits"* and they chatted together as if they were back in the *châteaux* of her first marriage. Unlike with the upper bourgeoisie of the Leofric, I now had my first taste of life in the castles. Servants and aristos alike lived in a totally different world to the one which I had experienced until now.

In those days the entire train was loaded onto the ferry and the carriages were shaken to death during the shunting. After that it was the clatter of chains in the wheels as they prepared for a particularly rough crossing that night. Rough would be putting it mildly and after less than half way across the Channel I spent the rest of the crossing in a praying position in the toilets. On our arrival in France and on firm ground again I was just dozing off when we were suddenly disturbed by the *"Douane"* the French customs. Amongst the formalities on the declaration sheet, which we had filled in at the start of our journey at Victoria, we had forgotten to include the dog. Evidently they considered it was an object of value, so we had to pay fifteen francs duty on the dog plus a fine of another two hundred francs for attempted smuggling.

During the remainder of the trip to Paris Françoise was fast asleep so I slightly raised the blinds and spent the following hours with my nose pressed against the window, scouring the countryside for the slightest sign which might convince me I was really in France. I still could not believe this was true. All I could see was a classroom with Madame Julien whacking us with her ruler and screaming at us because we were worthless as far as French was concerned. The only thing I did see was a sheep shed in a field in the middle of nowhere with a publicity sign on one side advertising *"Byrrh"* an aperitif which was popular at the time. As for aperitif, the sign reminded me I could not even spell that properly before I went to work at the Leofric and now, only six months later, here I was in France. I finally went to sleep dreaming of Sydney Carton in Dickens' *Tale of Two Cities*; I was following in his footsteps between London and Paris.

It was stifling hot in our cabin but Françoise said it was normal, only the primitive English had never heard of central heating. The steward brought us our breakfast and this was the very first time in my life I tasted croissants, the typical French breakfast pastry. Françoise said they were greasy and uneatable but for me, they were delicious. They came aboard when the train had arrived at Dunkirk and they were French, which was all that counted for me.

When the train reached its destination at the Gare du Nord it was a wilderness and I was totally lost. Paris stations have nothing in common with London stations. We made our way to the taxis and Françoise gave as our destination la rue Caumartin. If she had said, "the far side of the moon" it would have been all the same to me. Just as in the train, I pressed my nose against the window of the taxi, lapping up every shop front and traffic sign along the route to convince myself I was really in Paris. We stopped off at the Hotel Astor, which had once been the residence of King Edward VII during the "entente cordiale" when France and Britain patched up their differences, but, being full, they could not take us. A few yards further along was the Hotel St Petersburg, so we settled in there. It was immediately opposite her mother's property of le square de l' Opéra. After a night like that it took us the entire morning to recuperate, but in the afternoon we entered the square which her grandfather had built and took the lift to the fifth floor of number two. Then we mounted the stairs to the sixth floor and the servants' quarters. It was a very "chic" district, so servants' quarters still existed.

There I met "Ninette", Madame Emilienne Meylan, *épouse* Hornbostel, who had been Françoise's first lesbian mistress after being initiated by her children's nanny at the age of eight. She was an adorable short little tubby woman and typical Parisienne. She had married a first war aviator at the age of 14, which was the minimum age at the time. After hostilities had ceased he became a director in one of the big sugar importers and spent a lot of time in Casablanca. While her husband was negotiating sugar Ninette lived in the harem, where she learnt Arabic and lesbianism. After a while they divorced, she finally decided she preferred women to men. Before her retirement she had made *"poupées"* for the big Paris fashion houses in the days when it was the custom that when a woman bought one of the creations, the house would give her children an identical doll dressed in the same robes as the mother. After the war she became a tenant in the square via Christian who had introduced her to his sister-in-law. Little did Madeleine suspect that Ninette would seduce her twelve year old daughter almost as soon as she had moved in.

She must have been into her seventies when I met her, but when we showed up without announcing our arrival she seized hold of Françoise as if she had been her own long lost daughter. When she learnt that I had been the cause of Françoise's departure from London she seized hold of me, hugging and kissing me as if I had just saved the life of her Françoise, which I probably had. She spoke so fast and without the slightest pause, I had no possibility of separating her words. Even Françoise did not bother to listen to her. It took me another five years before I could begin to decipher her tirades.

At this stage I never met Françoise's mother, this was only to come about four years later in Normandy, but the old girl was so pleased to learn her daughter had left London for good she gave her unlimited cash for the time being. The first thing Françoise did was to seek out her former life, when she was the queen of Paris. We spent some time buying decent clothes, then finally one evening reserving a place at Maxim's, the number one restaurant of the day in Paris. The director, Maurice Carré, had set aside Herman Goering's table just in front of the orchestra which, on her arrival, immediately played "Lili Marlène." She was received with open arms. The queen of Maxim's had returned after a short absence.

We went to Maxim's, the most chic restaurant in the world, very nearly every night, and the poor little scruff from Dagenham did not feel out of place for one second. On the contrary, I was as much at home here with the aristocrats as was Françoise. As from my very first day when we went out swastikering in London she had begun to teach me, down in the basement kitchen, the correct aristocratic way to sit, to eat, to behave and, amongst other things, a disdain for the bourgeois' fish knives and forks, taking my asparagus in my fingers, eating my ice cream with a fork, and rarely using my knife, only in extreme conditions. She must have thought I was worthwhile material but this was only because I had received the basic fundamentals thanks to Baron Forte back in Coventry. In my two months at the Leofric, instead of reproaching the uneducated behaviour of my youth, and I made many ignorant errors there, he had corrected my unlettered stupidity and had begun to initiate me into a parallel world, without my realising what he was up to. I might have been stupid but I did realise Dagenham was no longer the centre of the world and that in reality I knew nothing in life. I had to start from rock bottom. There were valuable lessons to be learnt. Maybe he did have something in mind when he proposed I should work for him. Maybe I should have taken him up on his offer but I was still too stupid and inexperienced to realise the possibilities he had thrown down in front of me.

Even though Madeleine Dior was funding Françoise, she drew certain limits. She agreed to re-establish her daughter, but on the condition she became a ward of court with her notary, Maître Paul Jourdan in the rue St Martin, to be nominated as her legal administrator. Françoise accepted and Madeleine accredited her with a generous share in the family estate business, which guaranteed her a decent fixed income. Living at the hotel was expensive, so eventually we had to move out. Before she had left France to marry the NSM Françoise had accumulated a small following in France by placing ads in the right wing newspaper *"Rivarol"*, and one of her contacts was a certain Denis Travers who lived in Nice. I had already met him at the NSM while he was on holiday in London before I left for Coventry, so we were no strangers to each other. He was a youngster of about the same age as me, whose parents were working in the postal service in the ex-colony of the Ivory Coast.

The Easter weekend we took a Caravelle, the first aircraft I was ever to see in my life, from Orly to Nice. As usual in France there was a general transport strike on for the holiday period, but finally, during the afternoon, we arrived at Nice-Côte d'Azur airport, then took a taxi to the Fabron apartment of camarade Denis. Only a few days after our settling in, Denis received a telegram from Africa announcing the death of his brother in a road accident, so he immediately took the first plane out to Abidjan and we were left alone in the flat.

Our life in Nice was a paradise. During the day we would lie on the Riviera beach, soaking up the sun. The first thing I did was to teach myself to swim and after only a quarter of an hour in the Mediterranean I had achieved everything which five years of Valence Park baths had deprived me. As the day wore on we would go to the Negresco for cocktails. I had learnt plenty of them at the Leofric and Françoise was surprised by my expertise in their concoction. Finally, and in despair, the barmen presented us with a different cocktail every evening as a challenge and it was a rare occasion when I failed to divine the ingredients. By night we would eat at the Negresco restaurant and as soon as Françoise entered in her long robes the orchestra would begin to play Lili Marlene, the same as at Maxim's. When we were not at the Negresco we would be at la Maison Rouge, towards the port, which was the second elite restaurant of the town

It was in Nice I was to first experience Françoise's peculiar taste for women. Along the seafront was the Hotel Westminster, which had a reputation for being a venue for widows seeking adventure. The old girls would collect their pension at the beginning of the month, go to the hairdresser, go back home to dress up in their best, take a taxi to the hotel, then sit on the terrace making one drink last all afternoon, hoping to find a young man with a minimum of sexual experience but a certain amount of cash in his pocket who would invite them to take another drink. After two days without success they would cash in their chips, go back to their attic and meals of cat food, and repeat the exercise the following month after the next pension day. They made an easy prey for Françoise. Some of them were quite beautiful even though they might have been retired, and without any effort she would invite them back to our apartment for the afternoon. For the greater part of them this was their first experience with another woman, but for them it made a pleasant change to Kit-e-Kat and, seeing as I was present, it was less shocking.

I was as happy as a sand boy because, contrary to popular illusion, although Françoise had an enormous sexual appetite, she was hopeless in bed. She really was the proverbial sack of spuds. She only came into her element when she was acting the masculine role with another woman; but apart from that you could have been equally happy with an inflatable doll which was capable of having an orgasm after a lot of hard work. The routine was she would court and undress the woman bringing her to the point of no return, and then it was my turn. I could do whatever I wished on condition the woman experienced no orgasm; for me that would have been a fatal error and I would endure her displeasure for the rest of the day. The woman's orgasm was strictly Françoise's role later on. She found it more exciting to have a sticky woman who had just experienced a hetero relationship and who still needed to be satisfied. To round off the afternoon I finally had to satisfy Françoise while she was still licking her lips. Tyndall and Jordan never knew the delights they were missing but I doubt if they would have been interested anyway.

Before camarade Denis had left for Africa he had introduced us to a few of his Nazi friends on the Côte d'Azur, who in turn introduced us to others. One in particular was to play a deciding role in Françoise's life and he was André Trochu, a self-inflicted philosopher who first gave Françoise the esoteric works of René Guénon to read. Until then I had been banging my head against a wall concerning my cathedrals but from that day onwards she suddenly realised I had been right all along, although Guénon's works were based mostly on imaginary underground creatures living in a parallel world under our feet with gateways here and there, while my interest lay with real life structures. She immediately abandoned a life of painting and poster sticking to concentrate on the mystical side of Nazism.

One day we received the news that Savitri Devi, Hitler's Priestess, was coming to visit us. Savitri was born in Lyon of a Greek father who had been sergeant-chef in the Foreign Legion while serving on the prison colony of Devil's Island and who had married the daughter of an English factory worker in the munitions complex at Saint Etienne. Her parents had beggared themselves to give their daughter a good schooling where she eventually finished university with a doctorate. Without going into her long history at the moment, she discovered she was a Nazi in 1932, because she had seen swastikas on the walls of ancient Greek monuments and deduced the ancient Greeks must have been Nazis at heart; but when it became obvious there would be a second war in Europe she found she could best help serve the cause by feeding stray cats out in India, well away from it all.

She reminded me of Alistair Crowley, the self-styled "most evil man in the world" who, at the same time as Savitri, decided he could be more evil safely in Britain during the war, after being expelled from Italian territory by Mussolini. All the same, Savitri's train was booked and we all met up at Nice Central station to receive her. Françoise had made me clean our apartment from top to bottom because, by receiving the world's number two Nazi, everything had to be perfect. On top of that, we all had the strict instruction that when Savitri arrived we would give the Nazi salute and say, "Heil Hitler!" When she did arrive everyone gave the salute, to which Savitri correctly replied, but I thought it would have been more appropriate if she had simply held her hand out and said, "Cross my palm with silver."

I even took a look behind her to make sure she did not have a kettle on a piece of string tied about her waist. So, this was Hitler's priestess. She looked more like a refugee from a gipsy camp, complete with the typical gipsy odour, which is hard to define. We took her home where, in the evenings after the camarades had arrived, she gave long discourses, vaguely insinuating she was part of a great secret Nazi plot organised by top Nazis in a secret hidden location somewhere in Europe but of which she could give no detail for the time being. A few days later she took the train back to Lyon. I was glad to see the back of her.

The rest of the time passed in routine: beach, Negresco, Westminster Hotel from time to time; and then, early one Sunday morning in October, there was a ring at the door bell. I pulled on my dressing gown, opened the door and was confronted by two guys, one pointing a gun straight at me. I calmly said good morning and invited them in, turning my back on the shooter. They looked at each other in surprise, then informed me they were police officers come to arrest Françoise.

To which I asked, as I was about to prepare breakfast, if they would like some coffee. They accepted and we sat down in the kitchen. Later on they told me they had often heard of the British phlegm (apathy) but this was the first time they had seen it in action.

When Françoise appeared they told her, much to their consternation, they were obliged to execute an order condemning her to four months in prison. She had been tried in her absence according to French law for posting enemy propaganda in Paris before she had left France for Britain. A few months before finally taking up residence in London she had been arrested one night in front of the British embassy for putting a sticker on the wall which read in English "Democracy is hypocrisy", followed by a swastika and the address of the NSM in Princedale Road. Although an armistice was signed on the 8th May, 1945, the Second World War was never completely terminated; and even today a state of war still officially exists between Germany and the allies. While she was busy in Britain arranging her marriage her trial took place in Paris, where she was found guilty "in absence" of distributing enemy propaganda.

Twenty years previously she would have been shot at the Fort de Vincennes, and under normal conditions she would have been entitled to one week remission per month; but as she had been condemned in absence she had to serve her full sentence. Monday morning at the tribunal the *procurer* (prosecutor) confirmed the condemnation and she was taken to the Maison d'Arrêt de Nice. On the way out, when we reached the top of the flight of steps in front of the court, Françoise spotted a press photographer somewhere down on the pavement and stopped dead in her tracks to give the Nazi salute. I was caught off guard and very nearly went head first down the steps.

After taking her to the Maison d'Arrêt the two officers took me to one side and we had a few beers together in a café next to the prison. They explained to me the press would be full of the story the following day and that Nice would become an unhealthy place as far as I was concerned. On top of that they would be unable to protect me. Would I like to vanish? They were the experts so I listened to them. At 5am the following day they drove me down to the airport but all flights to London that morning were fully booked. They arranged with the first airline flying out for someone to be booted off the plane under a pretext, and I took his place.

CHAPTER 11

Dagenham, Xmas 1966, Vienna and Munich

Nothing much happened after I returned to Britain. On my arrival at Heathrow the dog was immediately taken into quarantine, Françoise was equally under lock and key in France, so there was very little to be done. When we had left Britain I had travelled on what was once known as a "British Visitor's Passport" which, in those days, could be issued at any post office or labour exchange on presentation of a birth certificate and two photos and was valid for one year. I had obtained mine in Coventry because one of the barmen in the cocktail bar at the Leofric had been on holiday in Holland to see the tulips and the whores in the shop windows. He showed us his BVP and explained the routine, so I immediately applied for mine at Coventry labour exchange, dreaming of visiting France one day and meeting the sister of Forte's beautiful mistress.

While living in Nice I had exchanged my BVP for a full blue passport at the British consulate in their offices in rooms above the local branch of Lloyd's bank, somewhere in town. At the same time Françoise had taken out her first British passport. She could not produce her naturalisation document or her birth certificate and we knew of no one to countersign her application, but the consul said, "Don't worry, we know exactly who you are", and in due course we both had full thirty-two paged British passports. Xmas came and went as Xmas does. Finally Françoise was due to be released in February, so I gave a phone call to Ninette and then took the first plane to Orly, where I meet up with her at the airport.

On her release from Nice prison Françoise had spent the night at the Negresco, but the police had seized her French passport written in the name of Marie Françoise Suzanne, Comtesse de Caumont la Force, because, at the same time as being condemned for distribution of enemy propaganda, they had stripped her of her French nationality by cause of *"Dégradation National"*. In the eyes of the French police she was now a stateless person. Although the flight from Nice to Paris was a domestic flight they refused to let her leave the airport.

I arrived with Ninette, and the police showed us into a restricted area. Without saying a word to anyone, I slipped her British passport into her hand while nobody was looking and we continued as if nothing had happened. Ninette then booked us two tickets for Vienna in Austria. At boarding time we arrived at immigration control, where there was a heavy police presence ready to take Françoise away as a *persona non grata*, but on producing her British passport I have never seen so many jaws drop to the ground. We boarded the plane for Austria at about four in the afternoon. My long Christmas holiday had ended.

We went to Vienna on Savitri's suggestion. She was in contact with one of her participants in the secret underground Nazi plot, who could give Françoise some "valuable information and secret orders." The plane arrived at Vienna airport and from there we took a taxi to the mysterious camarade's flat in town. I cannot exactly remember his name; he had been a fighter pilot in the Luftwaffe and gained infamy for himself by writing a book about his heroic exploits during the war. Savitri continually pestered guys like this with a perpetual stream of letters saying, "Wouldn't it be wonderful if someone could hijack a fighter plane and shoot up Berlin?" and similar oblique suggestions, hoping someone would take her up on her offer. "Wouldn't it be wonderful if......" was her catch phrase.

When we finally arrived in Vienna the camarade in question was an old man sitting in an armchair, as if he had been in an old folks' home all his life, and was waited on hand and foot by his aged wife. I felt sorry for her. He might have been an ace airman in his younger days but in his present state he would have hardly been capable of flying a micro-lite more than a hundred yards from an airfield. He lived, as did the most of Savitri's top secret contacts, on the proceeds of their books, recounting their heroic war time exploits, with the difference that this one had actually shaken hands with Hitler. I was considered too low down in the Nazi echelons to partake in their secret conversation so I was sent out to take a walk in the snow while Françoise received her secret Nazi orders. When I came back Françoise shrugged her shoulders. I said, "Bugger off?" And she replied, "Bugger off." So much for her meeting a whole host of Savitri's top secret Nazis as depicted on the Internet on her release from Nice prison! On our way back to the airport I casually said he must have been the guy who had filled my father with bullets, and we had a good laugh. My father was a long forgotten dead hero, while this one would have been better off dead instead of being a shadow of a human being, rambling on about some heroic past while waiting for the undertaker to call. Come to think of it, he could not have been as old as he looked.

A few hours after midnight we landed in Munich and took a taxi to the Vier Jahreszitzen Hotel and slept until midday. While in Nice we had read about the up and coming National Democratic Party, the NPD, so when we finally awoke we decided to look them up. We easily found their office and were greeted by a staunchly ex-SS lieutenant named Walter Brandner who had been an SS guard in Dachau during the war. He was a "bitter ender" who refused to accept the war had finished. On top of that he loved beer, so we were brothers from the very start. When I last met him in 1992, while he was living in Ainring on the Austrian border, he still had a portrait of Adolf Hitler on his bedroom wall. He was a far cry from Savitri's secret old crony in Vienna.

We explained our situation and he found us a room in an auberge near Munich in a village where he lived himself called Söcking, just outside Starnberg. He had recently been elected to the regional parliament, the Landtag, on a Nazi ticket. The strike in France had grown every day and by the beginning of the year it had spread to the banks. We were stuck in Munich with very little money. The aubergist in Söcking had been a Panzer captain during the war and had been in Hyde Park POW camp with Walter after the war had ended. They were old friends but underneath Stefan Dietrich, the aubergist, finally told us his story. The Wehrmacht, the German regular army, would be "fighting like bastards" for months on end. Then, when the battle was won, the SS would suddenly show up and the SS photographers would arrive at the same time, distributing their snaps of THEIR victory throughout the Reich.

I loved Starnberg as from the very first moment when we set foot there. That day there was a thick fog over the sea and the typical Bavarian town lay still under a muffled silence. I eventually returned there twenty-four years later on a different mission. It is unrecognisable today. Söcking is only four kilometres from Starnberg but at the time you would be cut off from civilisation when it snowed heavily. Stefan's auberge was a large restaurant, with a bar taking up the entire wall at one end and tables strewn about the bare floor boarded room. Before the snow arrived the Zugspitze mountain on the Austrian border would come right up to the window. Today there is a motorway from Munich to Starnberg and Söcking is nothing more than a prolongation of Starnberg town. As for Stefan's auberge, it is a discotheque and a block of flats obscures the window from where we would look at the mountain.

As usual we lived on credit. We were so hard up Françoise arranged with Stefan to supply her with cigarettes direct from his reserve. They cost a few marks a packet and were destined to be sold in a vending machine and the change was included as a coin in the packet. We used the 20pf coin change to buy a bar of chocolate which constituted our midday meal. Finally, towards the end of April, Ninette managed to send some money from Paris, so we said goodbye to our friends and made our way to Munich station. We took a one way ticket to London on the night train via Oostende to Britain. Unlike the "Night Ferry," we had to unload everything ourselves to board the ferry to Dover. From there we took a train to London and a taxi back to my parents' house in Dagenham. Immediately we began to look for a flat somewhere in West London and eventually we collected the dog from the quarantine kennels at Chingford. Françoise was invited a second time to make another statement at Stoke Newington. Then, without any forewarning, one August morning the Stoke Newington police arrived at my parents' house in Dagenham to arrest her on charges of inciting members of the NSM to commit arson against synagogues.

Personally, I had a hard job to believe the charge against her of inciting to commit arson was true. I had lived with her as man and wife for over a year and in such a short time I thought I knew her better than anyone. If she had wanted to incite anyone to do anything crazy I would have blown up the Eiffel Tower for her but criminal acts were the last thing on her agenda. Looking back, the common factor between the Friday club torching their synagogue and the Saturday club firing theirs was Hugh Hughes. He was condemned in the first instance with Thorne and Evans but at the same time had been the leader of the Saturday club with Sparks. Somehow the police never made the connection. Hughes spent his sentence in D wing, Wormwood Scrubs. Since then, new evidence is coming to light that she had been set up. But I had lost Françoise a second time, except this time was eventually to have catastrophic results.

CHAPTER 12

Françoise in Holloway

Françoise spent five months on remand awaiting trial. I took out a rail season ticket from Chadwell Heath to Caledonian Road and visited her every day. My first task was to find a solicitor who would agree to arrange her defence. At first I went down to Yeovil to meet the solicitor who had handled the affairs of one of Savitri's friends, the eccentric Count Potocki who claimed he was the King of Poland. I learnt more about him later. In turn the attorney put me into contact with his London agent in Croydon, Mr Proctor. This was the first time I had seen the interior of a solicitor's office and my first impression was one of dismay.

The room was dark, filing cabinets on every wall, exactly the same as in the traffic census offices but with an elderly "professor" styled old boy puffing a pipe, sitting beside a youngster at a long table behind a whole heap of papers and documents strewn about in the greatest disorder imaginable. Years later I learnt that publishing houses resemble the same shambles. They read the newspaper clippings and Françoise's indictment sheet which I presented, then nodded to each other. The old boy took the telephone, calling the solicitors' service at Holloway prison to arrange a visit with Françoise. When the details had been settled he said, still puffing his pipe, "Don't worry, we'll see what we can do", then carelessly threw all the papers I had given him onto the heap on the table where they separated, provoking a small avalanche on the pergameneous mountain.

At first I was far from reassured, but after less than a week they expressed their surprise that Françoise had ever been arrested in the first place on such fragile evidence. Mr Proctor made several unsuccessful attempts to secure Françoise's release through a judge in chambers at the Chancery Lane courts. But public opinion, if she eclipsed to France, prevented any judge from liberating her on bail.

For the committal hearing at Stoke Newington they engaged, at a fantastic fee paid by Françoise's mother, one of London's top criminal barristers, Mr Beasley QC, who, in the magistrate's court, declared that at first he had his doubts about even accepting the brief, but after examining the evidence presented by the prosecution he could only claim there was no case to answer and demanded her immediate liberation. The same public pressure which had weighed against her in Chancery Lane obliged the stipendiary magistrate, who normally dealt with drunks and car thieves and was well out of his depth with this case, to send her to the London Central Criminal Court at the Old Bailey for trial by jury. Had Françoise kept this attorney she would have easily won her case at the crown court, however, one disastrous event was to follow another.

To begin with, although he was in prison himself at the time, Jordan was permitted to visit Françoise at Holloway. My distribution of tracts while working with Timothy White's had been more than fruitful and amongst the new recruits to the NSM were two young sailors from Western-Super-Mare who had joined the movement, only to have found themselves arrested along with Jordan for conspiring to distribute a racially insulting document entitled "The Coloured Invasion." This must have been a show case to discourage other servicemen from joining because I had sold many copies of this same leaflet myself outside the meetings of the Conservative Party's Monday Club and had never been arrested for it.

The brochure itself was nothing more than a sheet of paper, folded in two, containing choice press cuttings from the *Daily Telegraph*, complete with their dates of publication in the newspaper and which put immigration into a bad light. I could never understand the reason for Jordan's visit to Françoise because their divorce had been pronounced in August and they were no longer married. Having been cited as co-respondent, I had also received a copy of the decree. During this visit he persuaded Françoise to dismiss her legal team and engage one of his own acquaintances from Birmingham, a certain George Brown, who eventually made an absolute and thorough mess of her hearing at the Old Bailey. I have no idea what went on while the jury was deliberating the affair but they were out for several hours. The Stoke Newington police I chatted with during the waiting period told me this was generally considered to be a sign in favour of the prisoner but, after several recounts, they finally pronounced her guilty on the sparse evidence presented by the prosecution.

As an afterthought I wondered if Jordan's manoeuvre had not been organised as a means of assuring her condemnation. Count Potocki was firmly convinced that Jordan was, notwithstanding his title as Britain's n°1 Nazi, in the service of MI5 and was paid to keep potential Nazis in Britain under control. His deduction came about one dark and stormy night during the few weeks which followed Jordan's marriage with Françoise, on one of the occasions when she decided to leave him. She made her way to Yeovil, where she took refuge with Potocki and his daughter in their royal palace.

Their palace was somewhere in the middle of nowhere and outwardly was a corrugated iron chicken house as used in the industrial breeding of poultry. Once inside and you entered the realm of the Polish court. Potocki had completely fitted out the interior, as if he was back in his rightful palace in Krakow. There remains some doubt as to his exact royal lineage but his elder brother figured on "Hitler's wanted list"; the list of people to be arrested by the Gestapo had the Germans successfully invaded Britain one day. A copy can still be found in the Imperial War Museum.

Count Joseph Wladislas Edmond Potocki de Montalk was a poet and confirmed pornographer, who gained fame during his trial at the Old Bailey in 1932 for his work entitled "Lament for Sir John Penis, buried in the Mount of Venus" or something like that, which was considered to be an obscenity in those days. He was supported by Virginia Woolf but was sentenced to six months for his poem. When Edward VIII was forced to abdicate he distributed leaflets in Downing Street protesting against the Prime Minister Baldwin and was arrested again. The writer Aldous Huxley paid his bail.

He was not particularly National Socialist any more than he was a friend of Napoleon; they had both invaded his motherland in the past but amongst his works figure his "Manifesto for Katyn" where he exposes the massacre of the Polish officers in Katyn Wood by the Soviets. Throughout the war and during the twenty years which followed, the Nazis were blamed for the massacre, while the British government hid the truth. Potocki was arrested for the revelations in his Manifesto and sent to one of Britain's concentration camps, known as a labour camp, in Northumberland.

During my trip to Yeovil a Polish waiter at the hotel where I stayed told me Potocki had ordered him to leave his job at the hotel and become an unpaid servant at his palace. The waiter declined his generous offer. Potocki became involved with the NSM through a chance meeting with Savitri Devi in London. It was Savitri who gave me the exact details of the following story while we were living together in Normandy.

One day Potocki was walking down the street, dressed in his royal robes, when he came face to face with Savitri, dressed in her Hindu costume. Their first conversation went along the lines of, "Who are you?"

"I'm the King of Poland. Who are you?"

"I'm a Hindu goddess."

And after that they became the best of friends. Savitri then introduced him to the NSM at Princedale Road. Fortunately their encounter took place in Drury Lane in the heart of theatre land where Savitri's friend Muriel Gantry lived, so nobody took any notice of them. Françoise felt at home in the royal palace, Potocki had all the trappings of a genuine aristo, but Jordan was fighting desperately not to lose his Danegeld; so, to recuperate her, he drove down to Somerset as soon as he realised she was missing.

In the middle of this dark stormy night he had no hope of finding the palace, so he telephoned Potocki to ask for directions. Potocki said he would call back after consulting Françoise and asked Jordan to give him the number where he could contact him. He then checked up the exact location of the number with the post office operator and discovered it belonged to a lieutenant-colonel who lived nearby; I've forgotten the name, but he was also a member of the board of governors of the Bank of England. If Jordan had friends like that it suggested more than a freemasonic connection.

Coupled with the fact that Jordan had been to Cambridge University, which is the recruiting ground par excellence of MI5, and on top of that he held a second honours in history which is MI5's preferred degree, and remembering how Jordan had given his friend Savitri up to the police at the Cotswold camp, along with several other insignificant incidents where Jordan had done more harm than good to the cause, this was enough to convince Potocki he was a member of MI5.

Savitri had eventually become a *persona non grata* in Britain thanks to Jordan. When the police arrived at the Cotswold camp to arrest the American Nazi, Rockwell, one of the accompanying special branch officers, asked Jordan if he had any other foreigners present. He indicated Savitri and brought her forward to the police officer, who immediately had her arrested by his colleagues. She was instantly deported. In spite of a certain false mythology, which claims she remained in contact with Jordan until her death, she hated him and never forgave him for this treacherous act against Nazism. Potocki came to the conclusion Jordan's role in British National Socialism was nothing more than to aid Britain's security services.

Savitri explained all this to me in Ducey, which does elucidate the mystery concerning Jordan's extraordinary permission to visit his ex-wife Françoise while they were both in prison and the reason for him persuading her to dismiss the one barrister who most certainly could have successfully pleaded her acquittal.

As from her first day of incarceration I had taken out a subscription to the *Daily Telegraph*, which was sent to her directly from Fleet Street every morning. Her other daily offering was her midday meals. Immediately opposite the prison amongst the first shops in Hillmarton Road was a small café catering to workers on building sites and passing lorry drivers which, apart from their regular clients, also catered to the prisoners who could afford to have their own meals sent in. I arranged with the two old ladies who cooked the most excellent food there to have vegetarian meals sent in for Françoise every day. She was not vegetarian in normal times but, under the circumstances, it was more in keeping with her Nazi image. The two old ladies later told me the warders considered Françoise to be a model prisoner. At least she would earn her remission.

On the other side of the road from the café was the pub called the "Holloway Castle". The name came from the fact that the main prison entrance in those days resembled the fortified gates of a medieval castle and could have easily been twinned with the prison at Angers in France. In a very short time I got to know all the regulars, especially one old timer called Alf who, like me, was a fanatical horse lover and racing was our mutual speciality. We knew all the horses and all the racetracks which, curiously, correspond to the cathedral towns. Between us we became one of the few teams in Britain which actually made a profit at the turf accountant's shop. Our favourite bookie was Bobby Cooper, no relation, who was further along down the Parkhurst Road. He used to give a groan whenever we came in and finally asked us if we would not like to give William Hill in the Holloway Road a chance to share his bad luck. These people, the same as casinos, are very bad losers and if the croupiers catch you working a winning system, and they do exist, you are out like a shot. Alf used to laugh and say the punters arrive at the racetrack on pushbikes and by bus while the bookies roll up in their Jaguars and Bentleys. If this said nothing to anyone why should we worry about taking our winnings?

Aristocratic as she was, Françoise did not inherit the aristo love of horses, although she would readily give them sugar, carrots and bread from the other side of a fence. On the other hand, her daughter Christiane excelled in horsemanship, which was probably the only gift Mother Nature had bestowed upon her and Madeleine frequently sent Françoise photographs of Christiane on her latest mount.

Much to her own disappointment, Françoise's trial was relegated to the Old Bailey n°2 court. In the criminal world a n°1 appearance was the equivalent of starring at the London Palladium, but her case was overshadowed by a Sinhalese businessman named Dr Emil Savundra who could be considered to have been the unluckiest man alive of the day. He was the living example of Napoleon Bonaparte's statement that, "One stone in the middle of the road can change the entire destiny of a nation."

Dr Savundra had recently opened a cut price insurance company named "Fire, Auto, and Marine", which covered almost half the vehicles on the roads of Britain. One Sunday, the BBC children's service broadcast a four part serial of Mark Twain's *"The Million Pound Banknote"*. The following day the entire country was discussing this fabulous note, and the press printed a copy of one of the seven notes in existence, adding that there were several hundred or so half a million notes also in circulation. One of Dr Savundra's young secretaries told her boyfriend that her boss had a half a million note in his safe and the boyfriend asked to see it. At great personal risk and peril of losing it she brought the note out of the office one midday; and the boyfriend, who just happened to work in a bank, immediately denounced the note as a forgery. Overnight half the vehicles in Britain found themselves without insurance cover and Dr Savundra found himself eclipsing Françoise. She was furious that an immigrant had stolen her limelight, at the same time admiring his ingenuity.

After the judge had passed sentence Françoise gave a Nazi salute from the box, for which the judge could have added a further six months for contempt of court. There was nothing wrong with the British judiciary system and he had probably realised, in view of his years of personal experience and the meagre evidence which had been presented against her, that her attorney was to blame for her conviction, so he let the matter drop. However, my life at the Holloway Castle was one day to come to an end.

The second deciding event at Holloway prison was that Françoise fell under the influence of a fellow detainee, a confidence trickster by the name of Betty Bowman, which was not her real name anyway. I had already been excluded from the trial but suspected nothing in particular at the time. Towards the autumn, Betty, who had just been released, came to Dagenham to announce Françoise's decision to break off with me. Lesbianism was the order of the day in Holloway and when one attractive young German girl accused of passing stolen cheques was found to be pregnant the prison joke was that Françoise was the father. When I first saw Betty I could hardly believe their relationship had been sexual. She was an old hag in her late 60's and worn out after many years behind bars. If she was a professional confidence trickster she must have known exactly what she was doing with Françoise, who made an easier prey than the widows in the Westminster Hotel. Françoise's major weakness was that she was so easily influenced and this defect cost her not only her liberty at her trial but was now to very nearly cost her life. Even Jordan had warned me, before we had left for Paris, that as far as Françoise was concerned the last person to speak with her was always right. Under those conditions, I wonder why he left her alone in London for such long periods of time. He must have been convinced I was homosexual, like everyone else in the movement had so presumed, and that I presented no particular danger so far as living with Françoise was concerned. Betty asked me to hand over Françoise's belongings and the dog and I sat down to wait patiently.

I knew Françoise better than anyone, so it came as no surprise to me when, in the following March, a post office motor cycle came up the road and a telegraph boy knocked on the door. It was a telegram from Françoise and consisted of nothing more than a phone number somewhere in the Channel Island of Jersey. I went along to the box on the corner of Green Lane and Walnut Tree Road and gave it a ring. On the other end Françoise had difficulty in speaking and I could not understand a word she was saying, and she handed the phone over to Ninette who was in Jersey with her. She was so hysterical I could hardly understand a word she was saying, but I did manage to decipher an address somewhere in St. Helier, and that she was asking me to come as soon as possible. I went back home, packed an overnight bag, and took a train to Victoria.

In those days British United Airlines had an office in

Victoria station itself and when I hurried in asking for a seat on the first plane out to Jersey the booking clerk looked at me as if she thought I was running away from the police. I was lucky, in five minutes a train was leaving for Gatwick and the plane left a quarter of an hour after the train arrived at the airport. The clerk telephoned the airport staff to inform them there would be a late boarding passenger and said if I was quick enough I would catch my flight. My single ticket cost £6. When the train arrived, after what seemed an interminable ride down to Gatwick, I ran to the check-in counter as if the Devil was chasing me. I have never been able to run so fast ever since. At least I caught the plane. The Vickers Viscount flew over the Cherbourg peninsular and this was the first time I had taken a low flying aircraft. Everything down below was spread out like a map. I wondered how on earth the parachutists at D-Day could have been dropped "by error" so far from their original destination and I began to wonder if they had not been sacrificed deliberately simply in order to create a diversion.

Towards the end of the afternoon I was standing outside Jersey airport. The taxi driver had a hard time finding the exact address because all Ninette had given me as instructions as to where Françoise lived was, "Dr Campbell-Young, Westmount." After enquiring at every house the length of the road, we eventually found a bungalow, well hidden in an alley behind the main buildings along the street. When I finally rang the doorbell Ninette hurried me inside. The small residence smelt like an overloaded swimming pool and I wondered what on earth was going on.

CHAPTER 13

Jersey

Ninette showed me into the bedroom, where Françoise was sitting on the edge of the bed crying her eyes out while doing her best to vomit on an empty stomach. She stood up, then fell back onto the bed. She had tried to poison herself with bleach and had changed her mind at the last minute, as many potential suicides are so apt to do. Ninette had arrived from Paris several hours earlier and, although Françoise refused any medical treatment, Ninette had managed to feed her gallons of water before sparking off the vomiting which had effectively washed out her stomach; but even so, a reasonable quantity had been ingested before Ninette's arrival.

We gave her water and biscuits until late into the night and just after midnight she fell asleep, snoring heavily. She was as white as a sheet but the danger seemed to be passed. If there was any necrosis of the intestine, the following days would be decisive and without pity. The whole house smelt as if there had been a first war chlorine gas attack.

Ninette explained the situation. Betty the confidence trickster had succeeded in alienating Françoise from everyone in her life, Ninette included, while at the same time was selling off her belongings, which included a valuable collection of antique furniture which was lying in store at Maple's in north London since her first arrival on becoming engaged to Tyndall. Betty had also procured Françoise's cheque book and had emptied her account of the revenues which had accumulated during her incarceration at Holloway. Betty had found the house in Jersey through an ad in the Daily Telegraph.

Dr Campbell-Young was a retired psychiatrist with lung problems who lived in Jersey for climatic reasons and always spent the winter in the Bahamas, renting out his house during the six months while he was absent. As soon as Françoise was released from Holloway she was parked in Jersey, well out of the way, while Betty returned to London, emptying the remaining cash which was sent from Paris and which was intended to help Françoise start afresh, before vanishing into nature. Françoise was left with absolute zero. It was only thanks to the ward of court order that Betty had been prevented from appropriating her capital. Much later I learnt this was her fourth suicide attempt.

As soon as Françoise was back on her feet, with no visible sequels, Ninette returned to Paris, but the troubles and strikes were still on in France and for the time being it was impossible for her to send any money other than that which she had brought with her. After a while the psychiatrist returned from the Bahamas, so we were obliged to vacate his house. We took a room in the Mountview Hotel, which was only a hundred yards or so further down the road, and where the manager's wife had an Alsatian dog named Timber which often played with Helga on the beach. As usual, we spent most of our time living on credit. Françoise had no real desire to return to Paris, although the nostalgia of her former life weighed heavily in her mind.

During our long walks in the sunshine on the seaweed covered beach she began to reveal her family secrets. She told me how on paper her father was Raymond Alexandre Jules Dior, the elder brother of her uncle Christian the fashion king but how, in reality, she had no Dior blood whatsoever. I already knew all about her mother's fortune, but now she told me how the Dior family had once been a wealthy Norman family which had made their fortune importing fertilizer products from Spain and South America, up to the point where Lucien Dior was made Minister for Commerce and Industry.

After completing his studies Christian had been sent by his family, against his will, to the school for diplomats and was intended to become an ambassador representing the French Republic abroad, while his intellectual brother Raymond went to the Sorbonne University where he first met Françoise's mother, Marie Madeleine Eugénie Leblanc, who studied international law at the same faculty. Madeleine's brother Albert was a keen aviator but had contracted tuberculosis in the days when the doctors believed Swiss sunshine was the cure. He died, which meant Madeleine would be the sole heritor to their father's estate. At the same time the financial crash ruined the Dior family. What with the horrors of the first war, where Raymond had seen his best friend have his head blown off beside him in the trenches, followed by the family's financial ruin, Raymond took to drink, hating the fact that, notwithstanding his family would be normally considered to be privileged, he was no more than cannon fodder. As a journalist later in life he wrote many articles and pamphlets condemning war which gave the outward appearance that he bordered the line on communism.

Christian tried various enterprises, including creating an art gallery in league with his "gang of queers", to quote

Françoise Dior as she looked
when Terry first saw her.

My grandson Jackinson with Sylvie at Angers castle

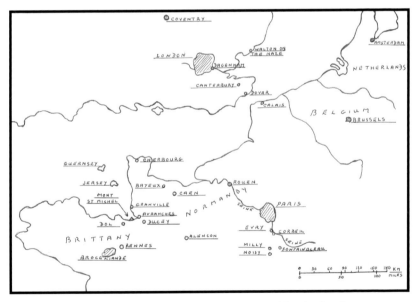

Map showing principal towns named in the book

Left: As a submissive schoolboy at 12 years old

Right: The rebellious schoolboy at 15 years old

Left: The author today

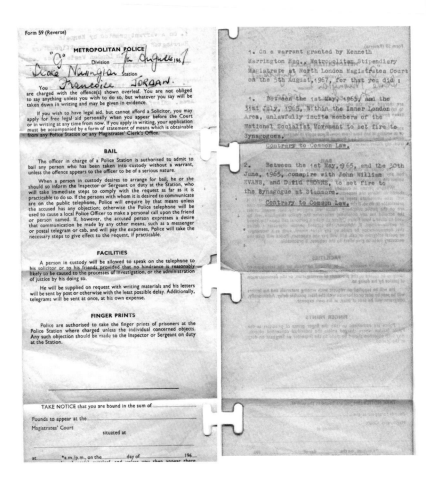

Françoise's indictment sheet

Christiane de Caumont la Force
age 10

Christiane de Caumont la Force,
age 14 at Noisy

The presbytery looking west

The presbytery looking east

Orchard, kennel, Françoise (left)
with author's mother

Fruit garden

Left: Savitri Devi at Ducey

Right: The Lupins, the inspiration for Twice Born

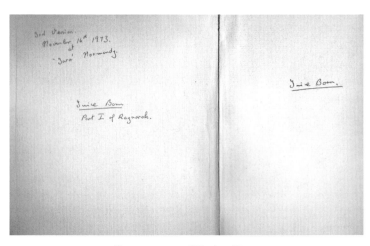

Cover page of Twice Born

The veterinary technician

Christiane de Caumont la Force
age 17

A list of dangerous sects in France

174 SECTES : l'inquiétant rec[...]

34 - HERAULT
Association culturelle alpha (Montpellier)
Après (Sète)
Aumisme universel (Montpellier)
Ecole internationale de la Croix-d'or (Saint-Jean-de-Fos)
Ecole internationale de la Rose-Croix d'or (Montpellier)
Mahikari (Montpellier)
Mouvement raëlien (Montpellier)
Sri Chinmoy (Montpellier)

35 - ILLE-ET-VILAINE
Arche de Marie (Amanlis)
L'Arbre au milieu (Rennes)
Anaf (Rennes)
Ecole internationale de la Rose-Croix d'or (Rennes)
Mahikari (Rennes)
Mouvement raëlien (Rennes)
Sri Chinmoy (Rennes)

36 - INDRE
Fédération française pour la conscience de Krishna (Luças-le-Mâle)

37 - INDRE-ET-LOIRE
Anaf (Tours)
Groupe Sri Sathya Saï (Joué-lès-Tours)
Mouvement raëlien (Saint-Avertin)
Temple antoiniste (Tours)

38 - ISERE
Association pour la recherche et l'étude de la survivance (Grenoble)
Association spirituelle Dhaidyakhan (Seyssins)
Communauté de la thébaïde (Rosbon)
Emissaries of the Divine Light (Velanne)
Les Amis de la confrérie Saint-Andréas (Saint-Egrève)
Anaf (Grenoble)
Centre Sri Sathya Saï (Fontaine)
Centrom (Vernas)
Ecole internationale de la Rose-Croix d'or (Grenoble)

39 - JURA
Shri Ram Chandra Mission France (Mont-sous-Vaudrey)
Centre de créativisme (Mouchard)
Eglise néo-apostolique (Dole)

41 - LOIR-ET-CHER
Centrom (Blois)

42 - LOIRE
Anthropos (Saint-Etienne)
Centre de dianétique (Saint-Etienne)
Centre du Graal (Saint-Etienne)
Groupe Sri Sathya Saï (Saint-Alban-les-Eaux)
Temple antoiniste (Saint-Etienne et Roanne)

44 - LOIRE-ATLANTIQUE
Institut des sciences holistiques de l'Ouest (Nantes)
Reiyukai (Nantes)
Anaf (Nantes)
Centre de créativisme (Nantes)
Centre de dianétique (Missillac)
Centre Soka Gakkaï (Nantes)
Mahikari (Saint-Nazaire)
Temple antoiniste (Nantes)

45 - LOIRET
Comètes-oxygènes-Le moulin du soleil (Autry-le-Châtel)
Imagine (Orléans)
Maha Shakti Mandir (Fleury-les-Aubrais)
Philosophies de la nature (Malesherbes)
Vital Harmony S.a. (Vitry-aux-Loges)
Cercle du Graal (Metung-sur-Loire)
Eglise néo-apostolique (Orléans)
Eveil (Huisseau-sur-Mauves)
Temple antoiniste (Orléans)

47 - LOT-ET-GARONNE
Association de défense des libertés d'expression dans l'institution française (Agen)
Fraternité Notre-Dame (Fréchou)
Cercle du Graal (Pujols)
Mahikari (Villeneuve-sur-Lot)

49 - MAINE-ET-LOIRE
Centrom (Les-Ponts-de-Cé)
Groupe Sri Sathya Saï (Angers)

50 - MANCHE
Cosmos, intuition-ailes (Granville)
Eglise christique de la Jérusalem nouvelle-Ordre de Raolf, d'Arnold et d'Osmond (Saint-James)

51 - MARNE
Cercle du Graal (Hertz-le-Maurupt)
Temple antoiniste (Reims)

54 - MEURTHE-ET-MOSELLE
Ecole internationale de la Rose-Croix d'or (Tantonville)
Groupe Sri Sathya Saï (Vandœuvre-lès-Nancy)

56 - MORBIHAN
Athanor (Néant-sur-Yvel)
Centrom (Montigny-lès-Metz, Volstroff et Thionville)
Ecole internationale de la Rose-Croix d'or (Metz)
Eglise néo-apostolique (Metz)
L'Arbre au vie (Spicheren)

57 - MOSELLE
L'Arche (Béning-lès-Saint-Avold)
Domaine d'Ephèse (Béning-lès-Saint-Avold)
Espace culturel être maintenant (Metz)
Mahikari (Saint-Hubert)

58 - NIEVRE
Energie et création-Enzergie et créativité (Saint-Saulge)

59 - NORD
Institut de psychanimie (Roubaix)
Association raëlienne du Nord (Lille)
Centre Sri Sathya Saï (Villeneuve-d'Ascq)
Cercle du Graal (Bouvines)
Groupe Sri Sathya Saï (Saint-Saulve)

60 - OISE
Château de Bellinglise S.a., Moon (Elincourt-Sainte-Marguerite)
Clé de l'univers (Compiègne)
Le Château, Moon (Sacy-le-Grand)
Red Concept Limited (Lasacquerie)
Sant Bani (Silly-Tillard)
Energie et partage (Saint-Sauveur)

61 - ORNE
Oxyon 777, ex-Harmonia (Alençon)
Société holosophique de France (Dompierre)

62 - PAS-DE-CALAIS
Mouvement raëlien (Boulogne-sur-Mer)

63 - PUY-DE-DOME
Association pour la promotion des arts industrieux (Teilhède)
Anaf (Clermont-Ferrand)
Centrom (Clermont-Ferrand)

64 - PYRENEES-ATLANTIQUES
Ordre apostolique-Therapeutic Healing Environment (Sus-Navarrenx)
Anaf (Pau)
Centre de dianétique (Bayonne)
Centrom (Gelos)

66 - PYRENEES-ORIENTALES
Les Jardins de la vie (Argelès-sur-Mer)
Ordre du lys et de l'aigle (Perpignan)
Ecole internationale de la Rose-Croix d'or (Perpignan)
Mahikari (Perpignan)

67 - BAS-RHIN
Anaf (Strasbourg)
Centre de créativisme (Strasbourg)
Cercle du Graal (Strasbourg)
Ecole internationale de la Rose-Croix d'or (Strasbourg)
Eglise néo-apostolique (Strasbourg)

68 - HAUT-RHIN
Centre d'applications psychiques - Raphaël (Colmar)
Anthropos (Mulhouse)
Centre de dianétique (Mulhouse)
Cercle du Graal (Colmar et Illfurth)
Eglise néo-apostolique (Colmar)
Groupe Sri Sathya Saï (Mulhouse)
Mahikari (Colmar)

69 - RHONE
Centre du cygne Djivana Prana, source de vie (Lyon)

Cintra and Athénéé theatre in the square

Madeleine's fermette at Noisy

Fermette and stables renovated today

Madeleine's 6th floor Paris
apartment in the square

Christian Dior's mill at Milly

Jean Cocteau's château at Milly

Right: The sinister corridor leading to Christiane's attic room

Above: Sylvie at Ducey 05.07.1978

Above: Christiane's inverted cross and butterfly brooch

Right: Market Place of Milly la Forêt

Left: Pigeon holes at the Père Lachaise

Above left: Mirleau and his new wife

Above right: Francoise's bone collection before being laid to rest

Left: Leblanc vault at the Père Lachaise

Mirleau's book

Dedication

Above:
The author learning firefighting

Right: Françoise remained
alive for the press

Françoise and Madeleine
together in the family vault

The author at
Raymond Dior's tomb

The author with the present
Ministre de l'Intérieur (Home
Secretary) Manuel Valls

Raymond, who detested his brother. Amongst others equally famous today the gang comprised Max Jacob, Picasso and Jean Cocteau, but the art gallery failed miserably after Christian contracted tuberculosis himself. Not wishing to appear to give charity to her brother-in-law, Madeleine bought one overpriced painting from the gallery and stored it in her attic, ready to dispose of it once the sale had become history. She had completely forgotten about it until many years later she suddenly realised she had a valuable Picasso upstairs gathering dust and which had narrowly escaped the refuse cart.

Originally, when Marcel Boussac, the "King of Cotton", took Christian under his wing, he did so without revealing his secret intentions to his prodigy. He had believed Dior would be making a loss, whereby he could offset his tax excess. Christian's overnight success came as a surprise to everyone. Christian had his own dream. He lived for the day when he could dress a woman completely from head to toe, from hat to shoes. When he eventually broke into the world of accessories, perfumes and *maroquinerie*, on the presentation of his first handbags he declared that his dream had finally been fulfilled. Much to his disapproval Françoise continued to wear "Shalimar", which she always bought in discretion at Guerlain's *parfumerie* which remained in the rue de la Paix after the main boutique moved to the avenue Montaigne, further down the road from Dior.

Christian's homosexuality presented no obstacle to his success. But many people were somewhat taken aback by the extremes to which he took his contradictory aversion to women. He designed his collections on paper and sometimes he gave a hand with the cutting but, when it came to the fitting sessions, he never touched the mannequins personally. The fitters would arrange the dresses on the mannequins and, to make the adjustments, Christian would use a small wooden baton to add the final perfection to his creations.

One day Françoise posed the question which still mystifies many people today: "Although the collections are guarded as top secret until the day they are presented on the catwalk, why do all the houses have such similarity in the choice of their cut, tissues, and colour of their creations at each different season?" Was there some secret complicity going on behind the scenes amongst the designers? Christian replied it was simply, "something in the air", which a good designer was, "capable of sensing as a natural gift."

During one of Raymond's drying out cures in a sanatorium, an old acquaintance from the Sorbonne, Valentin de Balla, came to visit his old class mates in Paris. Valentin came from an ancient ennobled Hungarian family which dated from the days when Hungary was unsuccessfully fighting off the Turkish occupation. They had kept their fortune during three hundred years under the Ottoman Empire, but had lost everything the day the communists had taken control of Eastern Europe. Before the war Valentin had been a playboy and, to atone for his sins, he frequently entered a monastery as a part-time monk for repentance.

In the absence of Raymond, Madeleine and Valentin, who were two solid pillars of the church, found the Devil's temptation far too hard to resist and, in the time as required by nature, a girl was born, to be called Marie Françoise Suzanne. Raymond accepted the situation, he had no alternative. In revolt against the hypocrisy of his religious wife and her monastic lover he became an out-and-out atheist. Although he gained a small revenue writing short stories which nobody read and freelance revolutionary articles attacking accumulated wealth in the newspaper *Le Monde*, Raymond would have been high and dry without Madeleine's fortune.

Françoise grew up suspecting something was wrong somewhere, but had no idea of the true situation during her childhood. When she was fifteen she learnt of the death of her mother's friend Valentin in a road accident. She remembered how he had taken her in his arms and kissed her as if he was saying goodbye only a few days previous to the accident, then she thought nothing more about it until, one day, Valentin's younger brother Borisz paid the Dior family a visit. Before and during the war Borisz was the Hungarian consul posted in Paris and had frequently visited Madeleine in the company of his brother. After the war he had smuggled the crown of St. Stephen out to the United States, only to have the Americans return it to the Soviets. The crown on public display during so many years afterwards was a replica. After his arrival in New York he took up a post in St. John's catholic university in Queens as professor of medieval European history, being awarded the title of Professor Emeritus on his retirement in the late 70's. Shortly after Valentin's death he had taken Françoise to one side and told her, "I am your uncle."

He then explained the family secret in full, adding the fact that he was convinced his brother's death was a suicide. As youngsters, when there were few cars on the road, they played a stupid game of driving at 150 km/h then closing their eyes for ten seconds. Valentin had not accepted their total loss after the war and Borisz was certain his brother had played their game, but this time keeping his eyes closed permanently.

At last Françoise knew the truth of her origins. She was a Hungarian baroness, with no claim to her title, living under a bourgeois name which was not her own. When confronted,

Madeleine acknowledged the truth. Raymond was left indifferent.

Two other persons were delighted. The first was Ninette and the second was the nanny Margot, who had tended Françoise since she was a baby and who had initiated her into lesbianism at the age of eight. Between them they began to formulate great plans for Françoise.

As a child Françoise was far from beautiful. Her natural colour was the same as her mother, brunette, and she had also inherited her mother's large nose. At the same time she had her mother's flat breasts. Between them Ninette and Margot persuaded Madeleine to let Françoise visit the beauty clinic, where the first thing to be arranged was her nose. The operation was successful but the result was slightly upturned, more than first intended. The rest, which included the hair colouring and breasts, which had left a scar on each side, followed with the passage of time. To pay for everything Margot prostituted the young Françoise amongst the lower levels of the aristocracy.

She was able to find her clients by using her contacts within the *"Association d'Entraide de la Noblesse Française"* in the rue Richepanse, now the rue Chevalier de Saint George, which is only a few hundred yards away from where Françoise lived. This association is a registered charity with the object of aiding impoverished aristocrats but which requires a coat of arms as the principal qualification for membership of the club. Her visits to the beauty clinic invariably coincided with her frequent visits to the abortion clinic. One of the club officers, Jacques de Ricaumont, who was to remain her close friend throughout her life and finally become chairman of the association, took her under his wing and taught her everything there is to know about aristocratic life and behaviour. Fifteen years later I too profited of these same lessons. I also learnt the difference between a snob and an aristocrat. The snob has to convince everyone around them that they are something which they are not. The aristocrats know exactly what they are themselves and that is sufficient for them. When everyone considered she was ready it was time to arrange a splendid marriage which would ensure her rightful place in *The Gotha*, the almanac of European royalty and higher aristocracy.

One playboy who was a frequent guest chez Maxim's was Robert-Henri de Caumont la Force, the nephew of one of France's ducal families and a count in his own right. Although he was a notorious homosexual he fell into Françoise's honey-trap, exactly the same as Tyndall and Jordan would do several years later. The marriage was arranged in due course and made headlines in the French press. Long before learning the truth, Françoise never considered Raymond to be her true father and always relied on her uncle Christian for paternal support. Even when Raymond died while she was in prison in Nice and she could have had a day out to attend the funeral, she refused the opportunity of a trip to Noisy where he is buried. It was Christian who gave the bride away at the altar at the parish church of La Madeleine in Paris while Raymond sat drinking in his favourite bar in the rue Caumartin. Just after her twenty-third birthday Françoise had become a countess in a ducal family and her name was finally written in *The Gotha*.

Unfortunately, Robert-Henri was not only homosexual; he was also a chronic drunk. He had been initiated into both at a very early age by the servants at the family *château* at Fontaine-Française in the province of Burgundy. After the marriage he was better off in the company of Raymond than his wife, and when the family spent their weekends in Madeleine's *fermette* in Noisy-sur-École near Milly-la-Forêt, they passed most of their time together in the Auberge d'Auvers Galant where they were known as "the two Beaujolais". Madeleine had bought the *fermette* on the suggestion of Christian, who had renovated a disused watermill in nearby Milly. At the same time his friend Jean Cocteau had bought the *château* at Milly.

Françoise hated children and hated even more the thought of becoming a mother herself. Just before her marriage with Jordan the French press asked her if she would be having children. She had obvious difficulty in replying yes and when further asked if they would be brought up as National Socialists she replied, *"bien sur"* – "of course", which was maliciously translated by the English press as saying, "all I want is little Nazi children." It was during this same interview she also stated that rank and file Nazism did not interest her, that she was not interested in British affairs, and that her objective was to form an elite in France. This revelation in itself is of the greatest importance. However, bowing to family pressure to provide an heir, she reluctantly gave birth to her daughter on the 4th November two years after her marriage. Normally the girl was destined to be called Florence, but, with the birth coming one week after Christian's death, she named her Christiane, in honour of the uncle she loved. On the day before Christiane's birth Christian Dior was to die a second death which irritated Françoise. He was receiving extensive press coverage but on the 3rd November the Soviets had launched their satellite containing the dog Laika into space. The dog froze to death within a short time because they had overlooked putting any heating in the Sputnik and Christian was instantly forgotten by the world's press media.

During her adolescence and early years as the queen of Maxim's Françoise had been her uncle's favourite, helping herself to his latest gowns in his boutique in the avenue Montaigne. She even boasted that her greatest rival, Claude Cahour, the wife of the governor of the Banque Rothschild who later became President Georges Pompidou, wore her second hand dresses. Their relationship degenerated as Christian's health slowly slipped from him. He was living on the worst form of drug addiction which any psychiatrist will pronounce as incurable, prescription medicine; which, unlike cocaine or heroin, is incurable once the habit takes hold of its victim. He needed some sort of medication to wake up, to have an appetite to eat, to stay awake, to have an erection, and, finally, to go to sleep. His day was one long series of injections, to which Françoise protested. His life was ordained by his *gouvernante-secrétaire*, who was the high priestess of his boutique. She decided his every move and at the same time procured a series of young men to satisfy his desires which, after one strenuous night in Italy, did eventually kill him.

Françoise came to the conclusion Christian was in the clutches of a plot designed to liquidate him while he was at the height of his fame, immortalising his name after an early death rather than letting him drift into oblivion. Towards the end of the fifties the trends were becoming more and more popularised; Maxim's had seen the height of the golden days of Gigi, an aristocrat's title was beginning to have less impact, and, in general, the decline which finally terminated with "Flower Power", the abolition of the Lord Chamberlain's blue pencil and Carnaby Street had begun. The days of the palaces and salons were coming to a rapid end, and Christian Dior would never have been able to accept this. His untimely death at the age of 52 would make his name live forever. He was succeeded by Yves St Laurent, who in turn handed over the reins to Marc Bohan, both flexible to the changes on the fashion scene.

As soon as she realised what was happening to her uncle, Françoise began making a fuss, which developed into outright scandals, until Christian was obliged to totally forbid her entry onto his premises. Normally she would have been his successor and, when he changed his will, this was the final act which convinced her about the existence of a plot. Under French inheritance law it should have been his brother Raymond who inherited his personal fortune, but they hated each other since childhood. Christian's earliest memory of their family manor in Granville was of Raymond locking him down in the cellar underneath the house, before scouring the garden for vermin and insects which he would push under the door to terrify him.

On the rare occasions when they found themselves together later in life it would always terminate in a heated row, with Raymond calling his brother, "You filthy queer" while Christian would reply with, "You impotent drunk." Raymond was disinherited in favour of Françoise, until she interfered with Christian's private life. At this point Françoise made no connection between the fact that both the high priestess of the rue Montaigne and the doctor who administered the injections happened to be Jewish.

The marriage between Robert-Henri and Françoise never really took off the ground as from the very beginning. Françoise had achieved her objective of seeing her name in its rightful place in *The Gotha* and the only point they had in common was their love of the Paris night life; but after the birth of Christiane, even that turned sour. Françoise began frequenting a series of lovers which she found amongst the diplomatic corps that had made Maxim's their after work venue. Her favourites were the Belgian ambassador, Baron Marcel-Henri Jaspar; the Cuban ambassador, Hector d'Ayala, who was to chose to remain in Paris after Castro had seized power back home; and, the one who was to influence her the most, the Swedish ambassador, Ragnar Kumlin, who introduced her to Nazism. Her memories of the Belgian embassy included making love on the balcony with His Excellency Jaspar while a riot was going on in the street below, with the crowd screaming for the end of the Belgian government. At the same time, down in the cellar, the Belgian secret police were already preparing the chains on the walls for the dissident leaders.

Jaspar was the eventual cause of their divorce. One day it had been raining heavily and Françoise was late home. She gave the excuse that there were no taxis free, but Robert-Henri noticed her shoes were spotless. He said, "You didn't walk home, you've spent the afternoon with Jaspar." He immediately demanded a divorce, after only four years of marriage, which they presented as "by mutual consent" to avoid a scandal.

During the war Ragnar Kumlin had been the liaison agent between the Nazis and the allies and, as an avid aviator, had been a great personal friend of Herman Goering. In 1940, he had asked for a transfer from his position in the Foreign Ministry trade department for foreign relations to the political department dealing with Swedish-German affairs. He said that if the Soviet Union was on the winning side, unlike after the first war, Sweden and Finland risked foreign occupation and it was he who took the appropriate steps preventing this eventuality. He also predicted the Cold War and Soviet domination of the Balkans.

After the war Kumlin was severely criticised for his connections with Germany. He was the chairman of the Swedish delegation at the Chicago convention on International Civil Aviation in November 1944, and, although Sweden was a neutral power during the war, represented his country in the Allied High Commission in Western Germany. In 1956, the 59 year old diplomat received his appointment to the post of Swedish ambassador to Paris; where he met Françoise, just one year after her marriage with Robert-Henri.

In reality Françoise's conversion to Nazism was far more recent than most people realise or want to believe. At one point in her interview with the French press she states herself that she has only become a Nazi, "since several years." During their afternoons on his sofa in the embassy in the rue Barbet de Jouy, Ragnar taught her National Socialism, which eventually became her personal creed; including the realisation that the central characters in the plot to liquidate Christian Dior were Jewish; hence it was a Jewish plot. For her this was the proof Ragnar was right about a general plot for Jewish world domination. He had successfully initiated her into Hitlerism, personally motivated as it was; and she intended to use Nazism in Paris as a means to avenge her uncle's death. Hence her statement that rank and file Nazism did not interest her and that her concern was to create an elite in France.

During our conversations about Ragnar, I had the sudden revelation that the only plotting in her head was not burning synagogues in London but Christian Dior's boutique in Paris. She wanted to use her Nazi elite to infiltrate and destroy the entire fashion house which she considered had been stolen from him. Her primary hatred in life was against the conspirators who had murdered her uncle. It was Ragnar who had denounced them as Jewish as a prolongation of his own pro-Nazi sympathies during the war.

Ragnar seized upon the fact that the main conspirators in the boutique were Jewish to further his own aims, whereas this was probably nothing more than coincidence. Most people in the rag trade, *"chiffons"* in French, were Jewish in those days. He converted his young and beautiful mistress as a means of assuring her ephemeral fidelity, but in her own mind's eye she would put Nazism to work for her. She had to become like Cleopatra, looking for an unsuspecting Nazi Mark Antony to do her dirty work for her in the avenue Montaigne.

The ads which she had placed in the right wing newspaper *Rivarol* was her recruiting program. But unfortunately the only Nazis who replied were either nostalgics, living on their short past when they had volunteered for the French SS division "Charlemagne" hoping one day the Germans might win the war, after which they would be given prominent positions back home, or hotheads with no commercial value as far as carrying out her plans were concerned. When she read of the Nazi activities in Britain and of their organized movement, she immediately fell under the illusion she had now found the elite she had imagined would very soon perform her retaliatory vengeance.

Her first deception came after bringing the impotent Tyndall on a reconnaissance mission to Paris, and her second deception finally destroyed her dream after her first week of marriage with Jordan's mother. She then became an unwilling prisoner of circumstances in Britain; impoverished by the very movement which she had counted on using to exact her revenge. When Ragnar learnt of her plans to leave Paris for London he begged her to stay, warning her that she risked losing everything, but his words fell on deaf ears. When we arrived in France Ragnar had just retired from the diplomatic service and, although he still lived in Paris, his doors were closed. He wanted nothing which might compromise his status. He died in 1979, without ever seeing Françoise again.

Ragnar and Goering both being passionate pilots, Goering had given the diplomat a Blue Max, the treasured first war aviation medal, which he in turn passed on to Françoise as a souvenir of their afternoons together. She in turn gave it to Jordan after their marriage; and he promptly sold it to have some extra cash in his pocket. It was also Ragnar who explained to her about Herman Goering's favourite table at Maxim's.

At the outbreak of war Madeleine evacuated her family to one of her possessions in the Basque town of St Jean de Luz, near the Spanish border. However, on the 25th June 1940, the Nazis arrived in the Pays Basque by the route nationale 10. Françoise's only contact with the Germans during the years they were in St Jean de Luz was when she contracted septicaemia and was dying. Her mother, being a millionaire, arranged with an SS doctor to treat her with antibiotics, which were unavailable to civilians at the time. There was no question of him saying, "What a beautiful little Aryan girl." She was still brunette, and as far as he was concerned she was a patient lying in bed with a fever and a pale green complexion who risked becoming one of his failures if the treatment did not work.

While we were in Jersey I realised that Françoise had completely changed in so far as her political ideas were concerned. While many people in prison take to some form of religion, generally either the Bible or the Koran, as a spiritual outlet, she had become totally engrossed in the mysticism to which André Trochu had introduced her in Nice. I bought an ordnance survey map of the island and we set out to explore some of the magical sites available.

We began with the Devil's Hole on the north coast and the wishing well conveniently placed along the route to the cliff. The well was no more than a bath tub, camouflaged with rough stones and protected by an iron grill. The only wishing behind this well was by the constructor, who wished as many tourists as possible would part with their holiday money. We found some dolmen in a field behind a farm, only to discover Prince Charles had been poking about with these same stones one year previously while he was doing some research for his archaeology degree. Far from magical, in the centre of the island at a strategic cross road a German pillbox remained as a vestige of the occupation, but the most impressive German construction must certainly be the Underground Hospital. It was dug out underneath a hill by Russian slave labour and still has the aura of death in every corridor. If I had felt a certain exaltation in my cathedrals on the mainland, I was pleased to be out in the open air once the tour of that hospital ended. Although I do not believe in ghosts, many children are suddenly gripped with a sudden panic half way through the tour, without any explanation as to their terror. Even the death camps, which I have visited, do not possess the unhealthy emanation of fear which this hospital continues to generate.

At the same time as Françoise's strength began to recuperate, her sexual appetite began to return. Her only conquest was a woman who worked in the dairy where we did some of our shopping. Otherwise she would be content to sit on a bench at midday in the Parade Gardens, watching the schoolgirls do handstands. We bought a few newspapers in the

French newsagent in the centre of town and whenever we went out for a drink in the afternoons it was invariably in the small bar of the British Hotel near the port.

Back in France the troubles were calming down and some money arrived from Paris. Ever since her recovery both Ninette and I had been trying hard to convince Françoise not to return to London. In the end she accepted our recommendation to live in France. Ninette had found a holiday flat in the small seaside village of Carolles on the Norman coast just opposite Jersey. To pay for our prolonged residence in the hotel Françoise managed to persuade the manager to accept a cheque drawn on her bank in Paris. Several weeks later in Carolles she received a letter from Jersey saying the cheque had no value in the UK banks but by then Jersey was behind us and had already been written off as a bad experience in life to be forgotten. Just after midday on the 30th June we took a taxi to St Helier port, where we boarded the ferry bound for Christian and Raymond Dior's native town, Granville.

CHAPTER 14

Carolles

The ferry docked at Granville and the tourists on an afternoon trip to France all disembarked and vanished. We were the last to leave the boat with our cases and a member of the crew invited us to wait on the quay while he went to find a customs officer to clear the baggage. Ninette was waiting just the other side of a barrier so, remembering our episode on the "Night Ferry," we waited until nobody was about, then slipped the dog underneath the barrier and threw Françoise's mink coat and six hundred cigarettes over the top. Ninette then discreetly withdrew from the scene. At the time there was no VAT whatsoever on Jersey. Cigarettes were sold by the 200 and the coat cost less than a third of the London price. Five years later I would learn how to make a profit on the tax difference but for the moment our main preoccupation was taking the taxi to Carolles and settling into the holiday flat which Ninette had booked for the entire season.

The first thing Françoise did was to contract measles and at one point I thought I was going to lose her. When I had the same malady at six years the standard remedy was one week in bed, the following week off school, and a spoonful of syrup for the throat until the bottle was empty. At 37 the situation was not the same. As usual she refused medical treatment, but I obtained some penicillin to protect her from a secondary infection during her weakened state. She recovered and we received the good news that Savitri would shortly be arriving. My heart sank into my boots.

A taxi rolled up and Savitri descended, along with eleven battered old suitcases and two antique typewriters which must have dated back to well before the war. Taking a lesson from Rockwell's entry into Britain by the back door of Ireland her objective was to return to Britain by the back door through Jersey. She stayed a couple of nights and in the morning we took her to Granville, where she boarded the same ferry by which we had arrived. I suggested we went into town to buy her some decent clothes then send her baggage the following day but she had the tendency to become angry if anyone contradicted her plans so I let Françoise decide the course of action. With her eleven cases and two typewriters, I thought if she wanted to slip into Britain discreetly she might just as well be waving a swastika flag on arrival. A couple of youngsters gave her a hand boarding the boat and we waved her goodbye.

The next day we went into Granville, to our favourite bar on the port. In the good old days the *"Lanterne Verte"* was the port brothel, but by the 70's it had become a fashionable café on the waterfront. On hot days we would sit on the terrace with a bottle of white wine and a dozen oysters, the rule of an 'r' in the month does not exist in France, and watch the Russian cargo ships arrive. Granville was still a busy port with much activity. When a warship docked the marines stationed in the *caserne* on the cliff were given leave and the whole town, shops, bars and all, was alive throughout the night. Towards evening we went back to Carolles, only to find Savitri sitting in the garden, surrounded by her hardware. She had been stopped on arrival at St Helier, spent the night in the cells, and put on the boat back to Granville next morning. On one page of her passport they had stamped an enormous black cross which covered the page and was dated and signed by the immigration officer.

She stayed with us for a couple more days before returning to Paris but in this time she managed to poop the bed, which she cleaned up in haste using bleach which left a large white stain in the middle of the brown striped mattress. She had no real conversation. When she was not making her continual allusions to the top secret Nazi plot she would be reciting some kind of perpetual history lesson relating to antiquity. She reminded me of the phrase from Gilbert and Sullivan's Mikado, "…..There's the idiot who praises with enthusiastic tone, all centuries but this and any country but his own……" As in Nice, I was glad to take her to Granville station and see her off on the train back to Paris.

During the couple of days she stayed in Carolles I learnt the virginity of Hitler's priestess was less due to ideology than of being a case of, "For the frigid woman chastity is not a virtue but a necessity." Three childhood incidents were behind her immaculate life. It was only on starting school she discovered she only spoke English with a smattering of Greek and could not speak French. When she did become proficient in the language with the other girls she equally learnt obstetrics in the school playground, along with such myths as if you use a toilet after it has been used by a man you risked becoming pregnant. After this she urinated standing up for the rest of her life. The second incident was when she came home from school one day a man followed her into her hallway and mounted the staircase behind her. At about halfway up he said, "Turn around little girl." Which she did, only to find him in full exhibition and advancing towards her. She dropped her books and ran. Lastly, one day in the park she was approached by a man who offered her a small religious icon if she would lift her dress and lower her underwear. She accepted and complied with his request. Then he asked if he could touch her. In return she demanded a second icon which he did not have. Suddenly remembering the man on the stairway she panicked and ran away a second time. She was wary of men ever since.

At the same time she claimed her vegetarianism originated along the same lines as Arnold Leese's objection to Kashrut. I doubt if a child in Lyon had much knowledge about slaughter techniques and her distaste for meat was probably inherent, rather than intellectual, as it is with many children. The Greek Pascal ritual involves eating a certain quantity of lamb. If you do not eat it you are not considered to be a worthy Greek. As a child Savitri detested lamb, I do myself, but, being a member of the Greek community, where she lived she was forced to eat some every Easter. To each one his problem, I suppose.

Françoise refused to visit the Christian Dior garden in Granville where the brothers were born. When the family went bankrupt the manor was sold and the town of Granville was the buyer. The manor was used to house officers from the marine regiment on the cliff but the gardens were open to the public. When Christian had made his fortune he asked the town hall to sell him back the manor where he was born at any price they chose to name, but the municipality refused. Christian swore he would never set foot in Granville again for the rest of his life. Françoise partially honoured his oath as far as entering his family property was concerned.

As the season came to a close we had to find quarters for the winter and we found a holiday house in nearby Kairon, on the banks of the river Thar, only a few yards from the beach. The house had central heating and the owner was prepared to rent it out between seasons. At the end of October we moved in but were seriously thinking about returning to London. At this moment there was an outbreak of rabies in Britain and the English press all carried the classic photo of an armed policeman laying in the grass on Clapham Common with a grinning fox standing behind him. In any case, there was a ban on the importation of live animals, so we decided while waiting for the ban to be lifted it might be a good idea for Helga to have some puppies.

A sturdy champion pedigree dog was found in Villedieu les Poëles and the puppies were due to be born towards the end of January. Helga made her nest under a wooden bench at one end of the room which took up most of the ground floor. In all, nine puppies were born. Somehow they contracted canine distemper before we could have them vaccinated. The vet from Granville, Dr Gamichon, managed to save them, but their resulting health made their sale value worthless. One did die, but before she went she sank her teeth into Françoise's forearm, sectioning a vein. As usual Françoise refused to see a doctor, so the vet sewed her up during one of his visits. We were stuck with nine dogs on our hands, with no hope of returning to Britain. On top of that there was a scare campaign going on in the press against Alsatians. Every day the papers carried a different story, "Alsatian bites a baby!" "Alsatian savages an old lady!" "Alsatian eats its dead owner!" "Alsatian rips the throat out of seven sheep!" And so on, in much the same way as there was a scare campaign against Pit-bulls recently.

During the long winter nights we were well occupied. In Granville was a bookshop called *"A l'Escholier Normand"*, where we bought up very nearly every book on sight which dealt with magic or esotericism. The rude weather in Normandy left little desire to be out and about much, so, between reading, our occasional walks along the beach while a storm raged, and the puppies, there was always something to be done. The puppies chewed everything in the room: the table legs, all the chair legs, the stair rails, anything made of wood became a target, all of which had to be paid for on the day we left.

Living in the countryside we needed a car, so we decided on a Fiat 124 break which had a space at the back for the dog. Here I began to realise how small events which had occurred during Françoise's life could influence her for the rest of her days. Two frequent visitors to HQ in Princedale Road were the Bartram twins. Eddie was a successful businessman living in, if I remember correctly, Berkhamstead, and his twin brother Danny was a tramp who lived in a doss house in Brixton. Danny was continually being thrown off the bus for not paying his fares, while Eddie drove about in a red Mercedes which he ostentatiously parked directly outside number 74, in defiance to anyone who dared to touch it. His business was a fairly large shop selling bric-a brac. In reality he was a fence, buying up rubbish such as chalk dogs and elephant table lamps that small time housebreakers sold to him for a few coppers, thus enabling him to make a decent profit by reselling them for a few shillings in his Ali-Baba cave. He carried a money roll in his back pocket. Françoise was very impressed by Eddie's Mercedes, so our car had to be red at all costs. No other colour would do, which held up the delivery date by three months.

She decided she would like to drive herself, so she took

lessons with a French wartime air ace, Roland Lacotte, whose wife ran a bar in Granville while Roland maintained his driving school at nearby Jullouville. Françoise was utterly hopeless at driving but after many lessons, and for the greater part thanks to her name, she did manage to obtain her licence after driving for ten minutes through the deserted streets of Granville. When the examiner wrote out her pass certificate he made her promise she would never sit behind the wheel of a car again for the rest of her life.

The price of an entire house during summer was prohibitive so, as the season approached, we began to look for a new abode. With nine large dogs this was not going to be easy. With our backs against the wall the only lodging free was in a tithe cottage behind a farmhouse in St Ursin, a few kilometres inland. Primitive would be one way to describe it. There was only one room downstairs and one up. As in all Norman agricultural homes, the north wall was continuous with no opening. In the west wall was an enormous open chimney where you could sit inside, the south wall had the door, with a window above the cooker and sink, while on the east wall was the staircase to a small attic bedroom. An old fashioned bed was on the north side of the chimney where, under normal conditions, old granny would remain until she died. On the mantelpiece were family photos of old marriages and baptisms, while above the chimney was a crucifix with a sprig of last year's Palm Sunday laurel gathering dust. A long table with a bench either side took up the centre of the room and the floor was beaten earth. Everything had the odour of burnt wood from the chimney. The exterior earth toilet was on the other side of the duck pond beside the cow stable. In all it was typical Norman peasant's cottage which had not changed much over the past few hundred years.

I made an enclosure for the dogs, but during our first trip to Granville they managed to escape. When we returned the courtyard was one mass of blood, feathers and ducks' heads, while the duck pond had turned the same colour as the Nile under Moses. The cost of repairing the damage was nothing; the farmer had been counting on winning a prize for his ducks at the coming agricultural show. It was then I had the idea of plugging my enclosure into the farm's electric fence system, which proved to be a very efficient way of keeping them in. Notwithstanding the loss of the prize ducks, his wife, Mme Lebreton, won the annual Farmer's Wife award organised by the newspaper *Ouest France.*

Ninette came to stay with us for a few days and was horrified by the conditions under which we were living. When she returned to Paris the first thing she did was to persuade Françoise's mother to buy her daughter a decent house. Just to verify the facts, Madeleine came to Granville. This was the first time I was to meet her. When she descended from the train Françoise greeted her, then introduced me. She looked at me in a way which reminded me of how Diana had first scrutinised me five years previously. She appeared to accept me and we returned to the cottage.

She could hardly believe her daughter had been reduced to this, especially after she had come face-to-face with the dead rat which I had remembered to place in the earth toilet before leaving to collect her. She agreed to increase Françoise's capital which had remained intact thanks to the ward of court order which prevented Betty from taking even that, but, she warned her, this would be the very last time she would ever aid her. If she committed any further stupidities, she would be on her own.

On her return to Paris she gave Maître Jourdain the OK

for Françoise to begin her search for a suitable house within a reasonable price limit. The search began and, after hundreds of visits, one of Roland Lacotte's wartime pilot comrades, a Monsieur Domien, who now had an estate agent's cabinet in Granville, finally found us an old presbytery in the village of Ducey, 12 kilometres south of Avranches and only 15 kilometres from the magic portal to other worlds, the Mont St Michel.

CHAPTER 15

Ducey and Savitri

The presbytery was a quaint old building which dated back to the days when the village was known as the City of the Montgomery, an aristocratic family which had fought with William the Conqueror at the Battle of Hastings. During the Hundred Years War, Ducey had been an English town. There were three *châteaux* in the lower village by the river Selune which still stand today, while in the old days seven priests and several novices administered the parish. The city once professed a convent and seminaries for future priests and nuns. The church stands at the upper end of the village, on high ground. The presbytery could be found at the end of a cul-de-sac behind the church but many inhabitants of the village who had lived there all their lives had no knowledge of its existence.

In August 1970, when we moved in, there were 3,000 square metres of grounds divided into the garden at the rear and an orchard in front. The rear garden was used by the previous owner for growing fruit and vegetables, while standing in the orchard were 120 cider apple trees and several varieties of eating-apple trees. In the garage were a cider press and three oak barrels. At the far extremity of the orchard was a wattle and daub building, once used as the priest's bakery and storehouse but which now would become the kennel for some of the dogs. Unfortunately, as they had grown older they had divided themselves into two distinct clans. On the few occasions when they were all together an uneasy peace would reign, until one of them provoked an incident, either by stepping on the tail of someone asleep in the opposing clan or by simply daring to lick an opponent's empty bowl after the meal had finished. All pandemonium would then be let loose. The only solution was to seize the free dogs one by one and isolate them before going to work on the assailants. Very often it finished up with me dragging one dog away by the back legs while Françoise would immobilise a second, hanging on to its tail for as long as possible before the third dog in the middle was free from the jaws of the other two. Once peace reigned it simply became a question of rearranging overturned chairs and mopping up the blood. Under the instruction of the vet in Granville I had now become an expert in sewing up torn dogs.

The house itself was beautiful, made of stone typical to this part of Normandy, and was all arranged on ground floor level with one part of the attic at the eastern end converted into two rooms. The remainder of the upper floor was empty attic. As with most of the Norman country buildings, the north wall was continuous, with all the doors and windows situated on the south side. The basic layout had not changed much since the days when it was occupied by a priest. The principal entrance hall was about two thirds from the western end. As you entered, a twisting wooden staircase leading to the attic stood before you with the door to the sitting room to your right, where the priest would receive his visitors. To the left were the living quarters.

The first was the bedroom, which was divided into the bed

space to the rear of the room, while the front was transformed into a boudoir. Continuing to the west, a small corridor passed in front of the bathroom and led to the dining room, which corresponded to the sitting room at the other end of the house. The kitchen led off from the dining room and was located immediately behind the bathroom. There were three chimneys, the dining room, the bedroom and the sitting room, but it was impossible to light them all at once. The strongest would draw upon the other two, filling the whole house with smoke. Ninette was a genius at interior decorating and, with the rustic furniture which she found in various antique shops, the presbytery soon came to resemble a small hunting lodge. The dining room ceiling was wooden beams; in the sitting room it was plaster but in the bedroom it was half a metre thick. The church was just next door and the bells rang all night.

To the north a stone wall separated the fruit garden from the new presbytery and the church. To the west were a few of the immediate neighbours and to the east lay the cemetery. When you opened the bedroom windows it was nothing but open fields beyond the orchard, stretching for five kilometres until you came to the next village of St Aubin de Terregate. This was perfect tranquillity.

The village professed just fewer than two thousand inhabitants and enough shops to cater for everyone's needs. Unbelievably, for such a small village, there were thirteen bars, all of which were doing a thriving trade. Before I could rig up the electric fencing two of the dogs went missing and reappeared followed by an angry neighbour, who had followed the trail of chicken feathers to the orchard. We settled in and a peaceful routine began. Françoise installed a chapel in one of the upstairs rooms where she would meditate each midday.

The chapel itself was a small square room with two lucarne windows overlooking the front of the house above the entrance and sitting room. The altar was an old marine chest, elaborately decorated by a seaman during his long oceanic voyages and which had found its way to an antique shop in nearby Sartilly. The altar was against the east wall, not for any specific religious reason, but because this was the most convenient place considering the lay-out of the room. Opposite the altar was a banquette with a mattress cushion where Françoise would sit during her rituals. Between the windows was a bureau where she kept her paraphernalia, which included an incensory, carbon biscuits and incense crystals, while on the opposite wall hung a large reprint of Bruegel's tableau, the Tower of Babel, between two wall lamps.

In front of the altar, at each corner stood two massive candlesticks capable of holding 550 gram church candles, while two smaller candle sticks stood on the altar either side of a small bust of Adolf Hitler. She bought all her trappings in Avranches in a repository, one of those old shops which have long since disappeared and which sold everything for the perfect parish, ranging from candles and incense to ornate priests' robes, altar cloths and trinkets to be put up for sale on the inevitable table to be found in the narthex, the area immediately inside the church door before you enter the nave.

Her ritual was simple enough. At midday precisely she would light her candles and incense, sit in a lotus position on her cushion, read a chapter of the Bhagavad-Gita, and then wait in all tranquillity for the divine grace to descend upon her. Somehow the Spirit always missed her out, but she had patience and was prepared to wait.

Life at the presbytery could almost be described as

monastic, except that before the autumn had ended Françoise began to make jam. She made so much of it that I still wince whenever I see a jar in the supermarket today. She bought up sugar and every kind of fruit in wholesale quantities before going on to things like beans, tomatoes, and liqueurs. She had learnt jam making in Holloway prison and loved it so much she continued to make the stuff for the rest of her life. On her arrival at Holloway they put her on wing cleaning, which she accomplished only once before complaining to the prison doctor that she had suffered twenty-eight miscarriages; abortions would have been the appropriate word. He checked the verity with her gynaecologist in Paris. After receiving the confirmation he put her to work in the prison's famous jam factory where, in a very short time she became an expert, teaching the newcomers her art. The other prisoners enjoyed working with her so much that production soared.

The other variation to the daily routine was she renewed her old habits from Nice. Frequently we would go into Avranches, where Françoise would pick up a woman to take back to the presbytery for the afternoon. At the Westminster hotel I could understand it was easy work, but in Avranches, as soon as she spotted a woman to her taste, she would be chatting with her for only a very short time before we were driving back to Ducey. She had very few refusals and amazingly, the ones who submitted the most to her charms were respectably married women, only too willing to share a dark secret to relieve the lifetime boredom of a middle class provincial agricultural town.

We had a bar which was probably better stocked than most four star hotels and in the evenings we would sip cocktails, either on the lawn while the heat of the day dissipated, or by the log fire while the cold winters dropped to sometimes minus twenty degrees. Françoise became quickly known in the village and Avranches, not because of her previous political antics, which were by now forgotten, but because Lucien Dior, before he became Minister for Commerce and Industry, had been a judge at the *Tribunal de Commerce*. In one of the back streets of the village stood the granary where, in the olden days each Friday afternoon, the *Tribunal Ambulant* would hold sittings. The judges and a *greffier* (clerk of the court) would arrive with all the trappings of a tribunal in their briefcases, which was all set out on tables on trestles before the audience began. Everyone in the older generation knew Lucien.

The first thing which interrupted our tranquil life was the arrival of Savitri. She had just retired and needed a place to stay while looking for something more permanent. She settled into the second room upstairs and began to write a book which at least kept her busy for the time being. A few days after arriving, she went down to the shops with Françoise and insisted on taking Helga's lead. After only a few yards she let the lead slip and the dog immediately, by cause of the similarity of the uniform, confused a passing *gendarme* with the postman and chased after him, biting his leg. The next day the *gendarmerie* wagon arrived at the presbytery, where Françoise and I were duly informed there was a deportation order out against us, signed by the *préfect* of Nice, dated 12th July, 1967, and we had three days in which to leave France. This in itself was curious because we were living in Dagenham on that date. The rest of the day was taken up at the *gendarmerie*, where we were fingerprinted and photographed, had our statements taken and were then released, with the strict order to return with our suitcases before the end of the third day. We immediately packed a few things and went to Paris, where we spent the rest of the night at Ninette's flat.

Early next morning we were in the chambers of Maître Jean-Louis Tixier-Vignancour in the boulevard Raspail. Everyone in France knew his name. He was the avocat who had defended colonel Bastien-Thiry after his abortive attempt to assassinate Général de Gaulle at the Petit Clamart in 1962. DeGaulle had the colonel shot in the fort d'Ivry seven months later. In 1965, Tixie had stood as extreme right wing candidate against de Gaulle in the presidential election. He obtained 5% of the vote. In 1966, he defended one of the accused in the mysterious kidnapping and disappearance of the Moroccan dissident leader, Mehdi Ben Barka. That day he had us to defend.

Leaving his other clients in the waiting room, he led us by a back door down to a battered old Volkswagen and, although it was a Saturday, drove us to the side entrance of the Ministère de l'Intérieur, the Home Office, in the place de Beauveau. There are armed guards outside all the major ministries in Paris and parking is strictly forbidden anywhere near them, but Tixie asked the police on duty to look after his car and told us to wait for him there. After half an hour he reappeared, drove us back to his chambers and told us to return to Ducey and forget everything. Our deportation orders had been "slipped into a drawer", to use the French technical expression.

Our first port of call back in Ducey was the *gendarmerie*, where we asked if they had received a call from the ministry. For the time being they had no news but by the end of the third day, instead of escorting us to Calais, we were left in peace. Savitri, on the other hand, looked less pleased to see us. She had imagined having the presbytery all to herself, where she could convert it into a secret Nazi headquarters and fill the place up with cats. I had confirmation of the latter because three weeks after the incident when the lorry arrived to deliver the dog food (we ordered in bulk with kennel status and prices), the driver unloaded a thousand tins of Kit-e-Kat. Before leaving for Paris I had given Savitri the order form, asking her to complete it and put it in the box before the last post went at midday on Saturday. She apologised and said she had made a mistake on the form, which meant that a grammar school teacher with a PhD is incapable of differentiating between Kit-e-Kat and Canigou on a sheet of paper.

In all she drove me crazy, incapable of doing a single thing right, smashing all she touched. She had several points in common with the French king Henri IV de Navarre. Exactly the same as her royal counterpart she would chew a lump of garlic all day where any normal person would use chewing gum or whatever they chewed in Henri's time, and like Henri, she was filthy dirty. She never took a bath once the entire time she stayed with us. However, unlike Henri IV, notwithstanding his personal odour which must have strongly resembled that of Savitri, he had seventy-nine known mistresses, while Savitri had no lovers; which did not prevent her from having an unhealthy sexual curiosity. I discovered that her promenade with count Potocki in Hyde Park ended with her asking to see his penis, which he duly showed her. On several occasions she played the innocent with us and asked Françoise if she could sit on the end of the bed while we were having sex because she had never seen it before. At least she had enough sense not to ask me.

Another of her annoying traits was her endless chatter about what the Phoenicians, or the Huns, or the Goths, or a whole host of vanished civilisations did or did not do over four thousand years ago. She also wrote endless letters to supposed members of her secret Nazi plot all over the world and obliged Françoise to endorse them with her own signature, although she had no idea to whom most of them were addressed, nor in which language the letters might have been written. Françoise found it impossible to do her meditation and in the end we were living on our nerves. On top of that there was her continual insinuation about a top secret Nazi plot which never seemed to materialise. She did have the visit of one South African youngster on his way to Germany and they retired to the sitting room for a secret conversation. Françoise and I were still too far down the echelons to participate. Unknown to Savitri there was an air pressure hole in the chimney which led to the garage at the end of the presbytery and I could overhear the entire conversation. Apart from a few banal exchanges, the most important thing on her agenda was, once in Germany, if the youngster could send her a certain laxative which she could not find in France. When he had gone Françoise tried her hardest to extract some information from Savitri, who remained as silent as the grave. If the great Nazi plot myth kept an old lady happy, who was I to interfere?

Several incidents made me laugh. Savitri was supposed to have kept thirty-five cats and a cobra back in India. I can believe the cat side of the story. Whenever we were out together and she spotted a cat walking down the road minding its own business she would always come out with something like, "Oh look, a pussy meow. Do you think he's being fed?"

"How the bloody hell should I know?"

"Wouldn't it be wonderful if we could feed it?"

Meaning, "How about slipping into the supermarket for some cat food with your beer money?"

As for the cobra, one day I caught a grass snake in the orchard and brought it in to show Françoise. Savitri screamed and ran upstairs. I still cannot work out the difference which a grass snake and a cobra might represent to her. On another occasion we were driving through the countryside down some lanes. At the time there was only one speed limit in France: 60 km/h in town. Once you left the town boundaries, which were clearly indicated, the roads had no speed restrictions. The red Fiat with its double carburettor was capable of reaching 100 mph (160 km/h) in only a few seconds and with fewer cars on the roads than today I made the most of things. We were hurtling along down one tree lined lane going towards the Mont St Michel when, on reaching a particularly sharp bend, we came face to face with a flock of sheep on their way to the salt marshes. I muttered, "Oh shit!" while Savitri started screaming at the top of her voice, "Sheep, sheep, sheep, sheep, sheep," as if she was counting them one by one. I managed to stop within a few inches of the leading sheep's head but blood was pouring from Françoise's arm. Savitri had gripped her so tight her nails had dug deeply into Françoise's flesh. I understood it would be useless to think of counting on Savitri in an emergency.

In the end Françoise could not bear her presence any longer and we began to work out ways by which we might be able to persuade her to leave. Finally, after about six months, which still seems like an eternity whenever I try to recall the exact dates, we were sitting by the fire in the dining room with the dogs strewn about the floor fast asleep when she came out with her catch phrase.

"Wouldn't it be wonderful if……….. if I could join my husband in India?" We both sat bolt upright. There was no question of Françoise paying her ticket to Calcutta but we were definitely going to help her on her way. If Françoise had the money we would have been in the travel agent's office in Avranches within the half hour, but as things were we were living on the usual credit, paying the shopkeepers once a month when her revenues arrived. Now I knew how Savitri had gone three times around the world. She would encrust herself until the host body could stand it no longer and would pay her ticket to somewhere, anywhere in the entire world, simply for the pleasure of saying goodbye. Françoise had an idea.

Before she had left for Britain when she had placed a few ads in the right wing newspaper *Rivarol* looking for her Nazi elite, amongst the replies was someone from Nantes called Yves Jeanne, who Françoise had met on several occasions and who was the self-styled leader of a non-existent French Nazi party; although he hung around many French ex-SS Charlemagne personalities who were still alive at the time. Nantes being not too far away but sufficiently far enough away on the other side of Brittany for her not to make the return journey, we decided to bundle her off onto him. Françoise really insisted that she should never make the trip to India before visiting camarade Yves, it would be unthinkable. She thought it was a good idea and although camarade Yves was out at work all day we dumped her at Nantes railway station before anyone could change their mind, then rubbed our hands all the way back to Ducey. She had forgotten to take her small coffee saucepan which was sitting forlorn on the dining room table when we arrived back home. I put it on the floor and jumped on it until it was flat, then symbolically threw it over the wall into the church grounds. That was the last we ever saw of her. Her husband could not have been too pleased to have seen her either because when she did finally arrive in India, and I have no idea who had paid her ticket, he made her live in New Delhi while he remained in Calcutta, 1,500 km away. Our only remorse was that at Nantes station we had forgotten to say goodbye.

There was one further repercussion to the dog biting the *gendarme*. Françoise was in court at Avranches and fined ten francs for letting an uncontrolled animal out on the street, but a far more serious charge was added to her hearing. On her release from Nice prison she had been given a *"carnet anthropometric"*. This was a small booklet with her photograph and a detailed portrait description, so complete the photograph was not really necessary. On the following pages was a list of the French *"départements"* where she was forbidden to live for a period of five years after her release. These consisted of all the Mediterranean *départements* from the Alpes-Maritimes on the Italian border down to the Pyrenees-Orientales on the Spanish border, the town of Paris, and for some unknown reason or another, the Norman *département* of Seine-Maritime which included the town of Rouen. We lived in "La Manche" on the west Norman coast so there was no trouble there. The complication came on the following pages. Normally she had to present herself every two months at the *gendarmerie* of her residence to have them stamped. All her pages were blank. The judge gave her a warning and advised her to comply. There remained only six months before the end of her five years' probation, so over the specified period of time she duly made the three visits required in order to remain within the law.

After Savitri's departure life returned to quasi-normal.

CHAPTER 16

Man, Myth and Magic

During the following two years the routine at Ducey might have been monastic but it was far from being routine in itself or boring. Basically everything revolved around mysticism because Françoise was convinced there were hidden secrets to life and had her mind bent on finding them. She had read all the Greek classics and her principal interest now was with René Guenon, Julius Evola, and Gurdjieff; we had both learnt their works off by heart but this was not enough. The library in the sitting room was extensive and was accompanied by a collection of classical music which could have rivalled the BBC sound archives. For Françoise only the practical side was missing. I had experienced my very first mystical encounter at an early age, maybe eight or nine; and this had been followed by several other "revelations" long before my trip in time at Coventry cathedral, therefore I had the good fortune to go even further down the road towards the unknown before our arrival at Ducey. Although I was still at the level of a "curious" I realised Françoise had, except for a miracle, no hope of ever taking the first step in the right direction. She was far too attached to this world. Notwithstanding this handicap, I did my best to keep her happy and hopeful.

Normally we would wake at eight thirty, I would prepare the breakfast which we always ate in bed, then give the dogs their morning meal before opening the door for the cleaning lady who did the essentials for the day. The rest of my morning was taken up either by doing some shopping or by fixing things here and there in the presbytery; and in an old house like that there is always something to be done. For the start of her mornings Françoise would remain in bed reading. Just before eleven o'clock she would begin her make-up routine which lasted until about midday, then she would go up to her chapel for some meditation. When she came down again, the cleaning lady had gone and we took a light lunch depending on the season. On Saturdays my entire day was taken up in giving a hand to the gardener who taught me so much about Norman rural life, including how to make cider and drink the cider spirit, Calvados, without making myself ill.

Our day began properly during the afternoons. Sometimes we would go either to Granville or Avranches, while at other times the rest of the day would be taken up with exploring historical sites in the surrounding countryside. Our activities ranged from exploring all the sites which figure in the Bayeux Tapestry, visits to churches and magical sites in Brittany, especially the enchanted forest of Broceliande where Sir Lancelot was born and where the fairy Viviane held Merlin a captive until his death beside the Fountain of Youth, which does not say much for the properties of the fountain. His tomb can still be found a few yards from the "Stone of Destiny." There is also the sinister Mont Dol, once surrounded by water but now several kilometres inland, where the druids carried out their human sacrifices. Even on the sunniest of days Mont Dol appears to be under a perpetual shadow. Sometimes it reminded me of the German underground hospital in Jersey with its morbid atmosphere. It is possible to take a car to the car park on the summit but you must be an experienced driver capable of stopping and starting on the steepest of inclinations in a narrow street with no room to manoeuvre, similar to the road at Land's End, before attempting the ascension; otherwise it is best to leave the vehicle in the car park at the base of the mount.

On the summit of the mount you can find a Devil's Hole, similar to the one in Jersey. The legend is that the archangel St Michel was fighting with his fallen counterpart Lucifer, who he threw violently to the ground, forming the crater to be visited today. The Devil burrowed downwards through his Hole, excavating the tunnels which are supposed to link Dol with the Mont St Michel, Avranches, Granville and Jersey, eventually surfacing on the mount which was to bear the archangel's name. The Celestial Chevalier was so furious he made one great leap to capture the Devil and his footprint remains impressed in the granite of Mont Dol.

In contrast to Dol, the Mont St Michel was once inland and is now surrounded by water where the sea comes in, "faster than a horse can gallop." This is not quite true today but high tide can still be spectacular, especially during a storm. Whenever there was some money to spare we would eat in the restaurants known the world over, la Mère Poulard on Mont St Michel, les Treize Asiettes at Pontaubault, and the hotel Tourne-Bride opposite the national stables of the Haras du Pin in the Orne where the Aga Khan and the Queen would dine incognito after visiting their horses in the Haras; the restaurant is closed today. Although Ducey is in a lost corner of Normandy, there was always something interesting to be done.

I taught Françoise how to connect churches on a map following the lines of telluric forces and she was pleased to discover by herself a Carmelite convent hidden out of site but which could be predicted on the map simply because it had to be there. When we explored the site the building had no exterior sign as to its purpose. It was only by banging on the door we discovered its true nature. We were permitted to visit the parts of the building where the public normally had access, which included the "parloirs" where the families could visit their relatives who had chosen to enter into orders. These parloirs were even more severe than those in the French prisons. They resembled a telephone booth with two chairs on the visitors' side and a counter protected by thick iron bars separating the visitors from the Carmelite. For a Carmelite convent this was modernisation. Once upon a time you entered the Order of the Carmel entirely renouncing the exterior world, with the intention of dying as soon as possible in order to ascend into heaven. The crucifixes were also Carmelite, in other words, without the figure of Jesus, because, in the eyes of the superiors, the effigy of the Saviour was also that of a man. It might give the nuns some bad ideas. Although the place was, to a certain extent, creepy, I was as much at home here as in my cathedrals back in Britain. We entered the inevitable boutique where souvenirs made by the nuns were on sale. Françoise bought some embroidery which she placed on the altar of her chapel in the presbytery attic. Finally I decided although Françoise had no real spiritual inclination she had an extremely well developed sense of superstition which, in any case, is the motivating force for the greater part of all those who assume any religion in any form. Some of her mother's religious fanaticism had rubbed off onto her after all.

On the quest for some more practical applications of mysticism we visited a certain Jean-Louis Bernard Klingel-Schmitt who lived in a ground floor studio in Deauville, just opposite the casino. I had already met him shortly after my first arrival in France, when he lived in a small apartment in the poorer quarter of the 15th *arrondissement* of Paris. All I can remember is that the apartment was stifling hot and although Jean-Louis Bernard was a small guy himself, the room seemed to be entirely occupied by his colossal wife and oversized mother-in-law. There was hardly any free space to accommodate the five of us. Washing was hanging up to dry everywhere, which gave off a tropical humidity, while at the same time a cat and a bird in a cage added a typical jungle aroma to the already unbreathable atmosphere. His wife had made a "*boeuf bourguignon*", a sort of Irish stew made with wine, but she was not a gifted cook and I had difficulty in eating what I took to be dead dog stew.

Her husband was scratching a living as a fortune teller, or clairvoyant to use the correct title, working under the name of Bernard, and placing ads in the once popular monthly magazine *Horoscope*. Savitri knew him fairly well, although one of her contacts well versed in the spiritual arts had warned her that Bernard was a psychic vampire, capable of extracting the life force from all who came into contact with him; and on all accounts, never touch any Egyptian statue which he might present for you to admire, it was his spiritual magnet through which he would drain your soul. From what I understood the only thing Bernard was capable of extracting from people was money. He must have cried his eyes out the day when Françoise left Paris for London.

By the time we had settled in at Ducey Bernard's dream

had come true. One day, a half-starved girl answered one of his Horoscope ads out of sheer desperation. Her story was almost unbelievable. Her father was the owner of the "Halles" in Paris, the French equivalent of Covent Garden market in the days when it was still operative. At about the same time as when Covent Garden was delocalised to Nine Elms, the Halles was delocalised to Rungis on the motorway in the south Paris suburbs. I have forgotten the name of the poor girl but although she lived with her family in a luxury apartment in the avenue Foch, she was a true life story of a Princess Sarah, a millionaire's daughter slowly dying of malnutrition. Her nanny was appropriating every penny of her allowance, an act of Barbary which went entirely unnoticed by her parents. She sought Bernard's spiritual aid and comfort in order to ameliorate her sorry lot, something to which Bernard instantly consecrated his every effort.

He made her pregnant, divorced his wife and married the girl. She must have been well under half his age but this presented no particular problem. His new father-in-law was hardly pleased with the arrangement but he did buy the couple the studio in Deauville, a town he visited frequently himself in his private plane to watch his race horses at the local hippodrome. Once a grandchild arrives even the most recalcitrant grandparents have a tendency to have a softening of the heart but I have no idea how things worked out at the Bernards' home.

The studio was worse than sparse, with hardly any furniture and with one of Cyril Lord's old wall-to-wall carpets on the floor. The baby was at the toddler age but was stark naked. Bernard's new wife explained this was to give him free access to all the Earth's telluric forces. I was just beginning to think this was an unhealthy situation for a child, especially as the Bernards were violently opposed to any form of vaccination for spiritual reasons, when the toddler crapped on the floor in one corner of the room. Nobody bothered to wipe it up or to clean the baby's bottom. When it approached Françoise she managed to kick it away without anyone noticing.

I do not think the child had a name either, because Bernard never spoke to it at all while his wife continually addressed it as "Titi." I felt sorry for it, especially after Mme Bernard explained that when it grew up it would be receiving a private education with some kind of a sect based somewhere in France, working on the teachings of Stendhal. Françoise renewed her old mystic discussions with Bernard but I could see she was far from happy with the replies which had once impressed her in the days when she had the idea of creating her Nazi elite in Paris. Bernard rambled on about a new Genghis Khan who would rise up in the east and conquer the occidental world. By now Françoise understood this was nothing more than a rehash of Nostradamus. Otherwise his favourite line was ancient Egypt which, as anyone looking for a new idea to create a sect today will now tell you, was played out and worked to death years ago. He did present one Egyptian trinket but Françoise, obviously heeding Savitri's warning, made me handle it for her. I could understand this coming from Françoise but I never believed Savitri could have been so idiotically superstitious as to fall for such a tale.

The point of separation came when, during one visit, we were all eating together in the studio. Mme Bernard was still as skeleton thin as the day when she first met Bernard and I wondered if he was not starving her himself in much the same way as her nanny kept all her food money. She ate nothing.

When Françoise enquired as to why her plate was empty she let slip that she had an amoebic dysentery which she had contracted during the days when she ate crusts which she found in the gutters of Paris as a child and was now obliged to eat only special foods. I do not know how modern medicine has progressed but in those days it was not only next to incurable, but highly contagious. Knowing that she had prepared the food herself I very nearly dropped my fork; and when I had the opportunity to inform Françoise of the situation she was furious with me for not sharing the information before she had finished her own plate. We remembered how the baby had made an uncontrolled mess of itself in the corner of the studio, and that was the last time we saw the Bernards.

In view of the fact the girl was the only heritor of her millionaire father I presume Bernard's dream has finally been realised. There is a publishing house operating by using his name in Brittany today under the title of Editions Ergonia which specialises in esotericism, occultism, and philosophy; but from what I can see, although the house is still based on exactly the same lines of thought which Bernard propounded over fifty years ago, Bernard himself appears nowhere in person, if he or his wife are indeed still alive today.

I decided to take a leaf out of Bernard's book and, as time passed, I discovered the secrets of constructing and reading a horoscope, becoming an expert in the astrological science, but poor Françoise still had her feet on the very material ground. To keep her happy I devised a whole series of picturesque rituals but was running out of ideas fast. I could easily have given her a few real experiments to perform but her materialist attitude to life made this impossible; and any failure on her part would have thrown doubt over the entire mystic compendium, reality or fantasy.

I took out a subscription to an English language magazine which came out weekly called *Man, Myth, and Magic* and which proved to be a mine of information and inspiration. Towards the end of the series, in issue number 107, on page 3012, was a sketch by Maurice Sand entitled *Les Lupins*. The drawing was of eleven werewolf characters leaning against a cemetery wall chatting together under a new moon. A new moon does not give off sufficient light to illuminate a scene and most certainly does not throw shadows but that is a secondary detail overlooked by the artist. These werewolves were specific to Normandy but, most important of all as far as I was concerned, their cemetery wall was identical to the one only a few yards from the presbytery.

I immediately had the idea of writing a short story based on the misfortunes of an English couple on holiday in Normandy in the Bay of Mont St Michel. As my writing progressed the short story developed into a full blown novel, with the central theme being alchemy and the passage in time. I called it *"Twice Born"*, a title which in itself covers alchemy perfectly. When it was finally finished I sent it off to various publishing houses in London but after I had acquired an impressive collection of rejection slips I gave it up as a bad job and stored the manuscript somewhere up in the attic, forgetting all about it. However, I was neither surprised nor disappointed; the book had become so complicated that, to anyone who was not well versed in the Hermetic art, it would be totally meaningless.

One incident gave me a strange insight into the hidden side of Françoise's weaker side. One Friday afternoon the *percepteur*, the local tax collector, complained to her colleagues that she was not feeling too well. She said if she did not feel better by Monday she would see the doctor; and she gave everyone their tasks for the following week in the eventuality she might be absent. Monday morning she was dead. An insidious cancer had taken her life in the space of forty-eight hours. The woman was exactly the same age as Françoise and I was forbidden even to mention the event. On the day of her funeral we spent the afternoon in Caen, visiting the tomb of William the Conqueror in the Abbaye aux Hommes dedicated to St Steven, in order to be out of earshot of the curious triple tolling of the church bell typical of rural Catholic inhumations. Françoise suffered from the one disease worse than cancer: cancer phobia.

All this time we received regular visits from the French secret police, the *Renseignements Généraux*, who kept an eye on us simply to make certain we were behaving ourselves. This was probably because they had nothing better to do. My alien's resident permit bore the number 5 for the whole department of la Manche, while Françoise was number 6, whereas my current one in the Essonne is number 17037. The RG were friendly enough and, in view of the obvious change in her comportment, had even persuaded Françoise to apply for her reintegration into the French nationality. Unfortunately three incidents were to completely shatter our monastic life in the presbytery once and for all.

The first was, Françoise's daughter Christiane had just turned sixteen and, in view of the apparent change for the better in Françoise, Madeleine decided it was time for the girl to be reintroduced to her mother. The last Christiane had seen of her was at the age of three; and her only memory of Françoise was of her wearing a blue dress as she said goodbye, abandoning her into the care of her grandparents before her departure to Britain.

As the Easter school holiday began the arrangements were made and the old chauffeur Pierre drove Madeleine and Christiane down to Avranches, where rooms had been booked in the France-Londres Hôtel. Françoise and I sat waiting in the hotel bar which still had the atmosphere of a London club and which had been frequented by so many British exiles from the post-war independent Indian and East African colonies of the past, but who are now all buried in the English quarter of Avranches cemetery. In due course a battered old grey Peugeot 404, in a worse condition than Tixie's Volkswagen, arrived and the introductions were made. Once the luggage had been unloaded I showed Pierre where he could park in the private courtyard at the rear of the hotel, then took him sightseeing, a tour of Henry Plantagenet's former capital city which rapidly deteriorated into a pub crawl from one end of Avranches to the other, thus leaving three generations of Dior to remodel their family life.

Christiane was a real beauty. She was well over six feet tall; slim with large breasts and auburn hair which fell to below her waist. She had inherited her grandmother's nose but, unlike her mother, was more than content with the appearance of the aristocrat which she was. Madeleine dressed her in a style which could only be described as classic, but underneath there was something almost impossible to discern which suggested she had also inherited her parents' degeneracy.

I later discovered that, in order to remain a virgin, she had let herself be sodomised as from the age of thirteen and, at the moment she first came to Ducey, she was already having a lesbian affair with one of her classmates, Mademoiselle Villedieu, whose mother was a professor of music in the Paris conservatory. Françoise quickly found out about Christiane's relationship with the girl but it would be a while yet before she learnt of her daughter's leaning towards anal pleasures which eventually disgusted her. Right from the very start I had the intuition that Christiane was to spell trouble. My intuitions were rarely wrong and this was no exception to the rule.

In the evening we all ate together in the hotel restaurant before separating our different ways. The Parisians went to their rooms upstairs while the Normans returned to the presbytery. The next day everyone assembled in the presbytery. For lunch we ate in the restaurant of the Montgomery hotel, opposite the strange church at Ducey where the tower had separated from the main building during an earthquake sometime in the 1800's, then, during the afternoon, I took Madeleine and Pierre on a sightseeing tour of Mont St Michel, leaving Françoise and Christiane alone to make up for lost time. This they most certainly did. After a separation of thirteen years and after being together again for less than twenty-four hours, in one afternoon the forty-one year old Françoise immediately began a lesbian relationship with her own sixteen year old daughter. Nothing was visible from the exterior and it would be another two years before I would share her; but I did notice a definite complicity between them on our return from the eighth wonder of the world.

As from that day onward Françoise lost all interest in mysticism and magic and returned to her former personality when she was desperate to make an aristocratic marriage in order to have her name written in *The Gotha*, except now the splendid marriage she had in mind was for Christiane. The name of Christiane de Caumont la Force on the school books which she had brought with her for the holiday was too much for Françoise and it threw her back sixteen years to when she was the undisputed queen of Maxim's.

Through her daughter she would relive her past days of glory; but a second unexpected event was to suddenly turn everything completely and irreversibly upside down in the presbytery. Shortly after Madeleine and Christiane had returned to Paris, the postman delivered a letter from the United States. Uncle Borisz was to arrive.

CHAPTER 17

Good Borisz

On the 20th May 1974, Cardinal Jean-Guinolé Louis Marie Daniélou died under mysterious conditions. He was found dead in a Paris brothel aged 69. Born in 1905, the cardinal was the son of a French member of parliament, living in the wealthy Parisian suburb of Neuilly sur Seine. At the age of twenty-four he entered the Order of Jesuits, being ordained a priest at the age of thirty-three and being awarded a doctorate of divinity four years later. At the request of Pope John XXIII he participated as *"peritus"* (expert) at the Second Vatican Council, opened in October 1962.

Five years previous to Daniélou's death, Archbishop Marcel Lefebvre, former archbishop of Dakar, had broken away from the Church of Rome founding his *"Fraternité sacerdotale of St Pius X"* in rebellion against the *Concile Vatican II* which had been concluded by Pope Paul VI in December 1965. Daniélou joined Lefebvre and became one of his right hand men in the *Fraternité*. The aims of the *Fraternité* were to maintain traditional Catholicism, rejecting the modernisation of the church, which included mass being sung in the vulgar tongue along with many diverse attacks on the ritual which they considered spelt the end of the true faith. The *Fraternité* continued with the Latin mass, ignoring the modifications initiated by the concile and had quite a substantial following amongst the traditional arm of the church. This was a thorn in the side of Cardinal François Marty, the archbishop of Paris and head of the French church.

The *Concile Vatican II* was intended to have lasted for only six weeks, but a whole series of intrigues prolonged the reunion for three years and very nearly ended with the total destruction of the Church of Rome as we know it today. Underneath the *conseil* had become a power struggle between a branch of the bishops, the successors to the Apostles, who had secretly united into what came to be known as the Rhine Alliance, and the successor to St Peter, the Pope. The Rhine Alliance consisted of bishops from France, Germany, Britain, Belgium, and Holland who had united with the intention of democratising the church and destroying the papal omnipotence. Things got off badly from the very start. The Alliance sabotaged the committees which had been formed to scrutinise the various points on the agenda and succeeded in the rearrangement of the nominated experts, which suited their own plans in much the same way as an able barrister would rearrange a jury to suit his client's case.

The most important outcome of the *conseil* was the recognition by Rome that the Holy Spirit was present in all faiths and that every different religion was a path to spirituality; thus destroying the two thousand year old concept that Catholicism was the only true faith. Before the final objective of the Alliance could be achieved evidence of its existence was presented to Paul VI who took fright. He immediately scrapped the few remaining points on the agenda, which included the ordination of women priests and the question of contraception. Had the Alliance succeeded, the bishops would have been able to outvote the Pope on any ecclesiastical issues whereas Paul VI, in bringing the *conseil* to an end, retained the papal authority over the bishops. But by then, most of the damage undermining the Church had been done. In Lefebvre's own words, "The new Liturgy paves the way for Satanism in the Church."

Although the Vatican supported Marty, the Holy See was far from satisfied with the official police version of the death of Daniélou. So Borisz de Balla was called to Rome, where he was given the office of Devil's Advocate and ordered to carry out an undercover papal investigation. Contrary to popular belief, when a miracle is announced, the first thing the church does is not to acclaim the act but to tries to disprove the wonder. This office of Devil's Advocate was established in 1587 by Pope Sixtus V, and consisted of a canon lawyer appointed to test the exactitude of the miracle. With the passage of time the office transformed itself into a Vatican secret police and was eventually abolished by Pope John Paul II in 1983, enabling him to canonise his own favourites, left, right and centre, to further his own aims, at the same time leaving the door wide open for his own canonisation. In 1974, the Devil's Advocate was still a very powerful person to be reckoned with. Her uncle's correct name was Borisz von Balla but, during the period immediately following the war, the particle *"de"* was more appropriate.

The job was given to Borisz because not only had he retained many friends in Paris from his old days as consul, when he was also a member of the Masonic lodge of the Grand Orient, but because Madeleine Dior had a direct interest in Dakar. Her father had been one of the principal constructors of the cathedral and governor's palace in Dakar, and she had spent many years there in her younger days while Lefebvre was Vicar Apostolic of Dakar, later becoming Archbishop; and they were still very good friends.

Françoise received the word of his arrival with instructions to keep his visit a strict secret. From New York he took the most complicated route to Paris, by Icelandic Airways via London and Vienna. I had to be at the Gare de l'Est in Paris at 10pm to meet him and bring him directly to Ducey. Having never met him before I was given a photograph of a cheerful silver haired elderly gentleman, with details of the exact spot where we were to meet up. The only trouble was, when we did meet he wanted to begin work immediately. So, instead of driving directly to Normandy, we took the inner boulevards towards the place de la Concorde and the avenue des Champs-Elysées. Here Borisz expressed his disappointment that the most famous avenue in the world appeared to be in decline and that since his days as a diplomat in Paris the street lighting had become dimmer with far less people milling about so late at night.

We parked a few metres down the road from the restaurant Fouquet's and went in for a beer. Taking some paper and a pen from his pocket he wrote something down. On the pretext of going to the toilet he ordered me another beer but said something to the waiter who then led him to a back room. A few minutes later he reappeared and asked to be taken to Ducey. I later discovered Fouquet's is a venue for Freemasons and the mysterious back room has a similar status to a lodge.

The A13 Normandy motorway did not go as far as Caen at the time so, to avoid the traffic, I always took an obscure route via Evreux, Lisieux and Falaise. Once we were on the RN.13 Borisz asked me which direction we were taking. When I explained the route he asked me to make a detour. I was already tired after leaving Normandy that morning and could have cursed him but he explained that before the war he had visited the Basilique de Sainte Thérese at Lisieux with his brother Valentin; and he had been so awestruck by the beauty of the edifice he had made a vow he would never return to Lisieux again unless he was in orders. Valentin easily accepted the role of a part-time monk but for Borisz, he preferred the debauched life of a diplomat. Notwithstanding, he stood by his oath and always avoided the town where the 24 year old Carmelite saint had died. This meant a detour through Alençon and the lorry laden RN.12. I was already fed up him.

Next day he wanted to go to mass, so I took him to Mont St Michel, where four monks held the fort before the main contingent of brothers arrived from the surrounding monasteries to put on a good show for the tourist season. I knew Brother Joseph very well, he was English and at night he would slip out on his motor cycle for a few drinks in Avranches; and I could have given Borisz an introduction but he had to remain incognito, even there.

In all he was almost as much as a pest as Savitri had been. He insisted on saying grace at every meal, crossed the loaf with his knife and was horrified if it was ever to be found upside down on the table; insisted on fish for each meal on Friday, with mass on Sunday, up to the point where I started calling him "Good Borisz", and I thought he would have been better off if he had stuck to his first idea of becoming a monk. During the daytimes I had shown him all the sights between upper Brittany and lower Normandy but during the evenings and half the night his old life in Hungary would take over. He would take root in the candlelit sitting room beside the log fire while I plied him with concentrated essence of prune, which is a great favourite in Hungary, leaving Françoise lapping up every detail of her biological grandfather's life in the old country before communism had arrived and when her father Valentin and Borisz were little less than princes. Françoise did a tour of all the record shops within a large radius around Ducey, buying up every Hungarian, Russian, and Gipsy recording available. Borisz living in the United States meant he had very little contact with France and, during the time they were together, he initiated Françoise into all their family secrets because she was the last descendant in their blood line. If she had become infatuated with her daughter, she was now totally obsessed with the world beyond the Danube. All this time he made frequent trips to Paris. I would put him on the morning train at Granville, collecting him on his return at Villedieu the following day.

Finally I took him to Caen airport, where he took a flight to London and from there he went on to Rome to make his report. He was not really so much of a pest like Savitri but I was tired of his fish on Fridays.

One month later he returned. I have no idea what happened during his trip to Rome, where he handed in his report concerning Daniélou's death, but as we were driving out of Paris he said he did not care about Lisieux any more. He could not care about having fish on Friday either; and I noticed that not only did he leave the bread uncrossed and ate without saying grace, he even ignored the fact that sometimes the loaf was upside down on the table, something which I often did to test him. When I offered him the choice of mass either at the Mont St Michel or Avranches he said neither of them mattered and remained at home. Something very serious must have happened while he was in Rome.

Although the official police report that Daniélou had died of a heart attack while ministering to fallen women still remains on record, Borisz had discovered the Cardinal had been murdered and his body dumped in the brothel to blacken his name in order to discredit the refractory Fraternité. The person who had signed Daniélou's death warrant was a fellow European cardinal and his hatchet man, an obscure priest at the moment in question, is now a bishop somewhere today after a rapid rise in the echelons of the church. In reality, Daniélou, by originally being a member of the Rhine Alliance, in defecting to the Fraternité had signed his own death warrant. A few years later I ran straight into the obscure priest in a deserted car park near Chartres and, unless he had carried out his own investigation into Borisz and his movements, he could have had no idea as to who I was. But the way he looked at me made my blood chill and sometimes today I wonder if I had not had a narrow escape.

With his religion up in smoke the only idol remaining for Borisz was his aristocracy, which no longer existed. His tales of the old country completely dominated Françoise's way of thinking and by the time he returned to the United States she had become a 100% Hungarian.

Madeleine, Christiane and Pierre arrived for two weeks during the summer holiday. Françoise kept the girl entirely to herself, while I had to entertain her mother and the chauffeur the best I could. When they had to return to Paris, Madeleine was as fed up with Russian and Gipsy music as I was. It was then I noticed something had changed with Françoise. Although we continued to live on credit everywhere as usual, she suddenly seemed to have unlimited cash. She told me her mother was helping her out while she was getting to know Christiane and since I had forgotten Madeleine's last warning about money, I thought nothing more about it. On top of that, her usual bank was the Crédit Marseillaise in Paris, under the control of her administrator Maître Jourdain; but she now opened a second account with the Société Générale in Avranches.

One day Borisz made an exceptional trip from Austria, where he rented an apartment in Baden bei Wein in anticipation of his retirement. It lasted only two days. As usual I collected him at the Gare de l'Est and when he arrived at the presbytery he took a heavy parcel from his overnight bag. It contained a complete set of dinner cutlery in gold, which he had salvaged before the communists had arrived in Hungary. Françoise drew out 50,000 francs in cash from her Avranches account and bought the knives, forks, and spoons, storing them in a safe deposit box in her bank. When I asked her how on earth she had managed that she said her mother had found it to be a good investment. Like a dummy I believed her. I had no reason to think otherwise. She accompanied Borisz to Paris and, before the year was ended, she was spending more time in Paris than in Ducey.

Just before Christmas the dog developed a rapid cancer. Although Helga had been the mainstay of her life since she had bought her in Birmingham in 1965, this did not prevent Françoise's absence, even when the vet in Avranches gave her only a few days to live. I asked him to open her up by *acquit de conscience* and as soon as we saw her liver he finished her off while she was still under the anaesthetic. Even then Françoise did not return until a few days later. At the time I had no idea what might have been so important in Paris but this state of affairs was to continue during the following years. Before leaving for Paris on one trip Françoise asked me to make a detailed drawing of Christiane's coat of arms which she intended to give to a goldsmith who would make a ring for the girl. It was simple enough, a lozenge with unicorns on each side, the uniform colour being azure blue with three silver leopards, arranged the same as in the English arms. When I saw the solid gold ring on Christiane's finger it was splendid; but the thought never crossed my mind as to where Françoise might have found the money for this gift, nor how she managed to spend so much time in Paris.

Many years later after her death I finally discovered her secret. I would not have minded so much if she had returned to the prostitution of her teens. But for me, the cruel truth was far worse. While I had been writing my book on alchemy, Françoise, with her photographic memory, had been making a secret copy in French which she subsequently sold to a French cinema producer; the end result being the film *"Hu-Man"* starring Terence Stamp and Jeanne Moreau. I can put a rough date on the time when she sold her copy because in the film the *"oeuvre noir"* (black work) is represented by a reckless motor cycle chase through the deserted night streets; and although this scene figured in my original manuscript, I edited it out because it too closely resembled a similar scene in the opening of one of the French right wing author St Loup's books, which I considered might border plagiary.

I saw the film one evening in 1980, while I was watching television at Ducey. Before the film had finished I had already packed a bag and set out, armed to the teeth, in the direction of London, ready to slit the throat of whoever claimed to be the author of my original work. Even if I had spent the rest of my life behind bars I would have the satisfaction of being rightly credited for my book. As it was, after a tour of all the publishers I came back empty handed. If I had watched the film to the end instead of dashing out on the spot I would have seen that it had been made in France, which would have explained everything straight away. As it was, I had to wait for the advent of the Internet before learning the truth and Françoise was long dead by then. My only consolations are my rough notes and outline manuscript, hand written in two exercise books dated 16th November 1973, which survived because my mother had written them herself on dictation and had taken them back to Dagenham after one of her visits to Ducey. I found them amongst her belongings after she died in 1989 and they sit there in my bedside cabinet today, as a reminder that Christiane was not the only dummy under Françoise's influence in those days.

CHAPTER 18

The veterinary technician

I was seeing less and less of Françoise and was growing bored all alone in Ducey, although a few married women here and there were delighted to spend an afternoon in the presbytery during Françoise's absence. On the rare occasions when I did see her she was completely obsessed with Christiane, Hungary, and her plans to reintroduce herself into the Paris aristocratic circles. During one visit by the vet I asked him if he had a job going which would occupy my spare time and he asked me what I knew about cows. I was stuck so I replied,

"They kind of stand around in fields and go Moo."

He said that was not bad for a start, so if I would like to accompany him on his rounds he could teach me as much as I was prepared to learn. I could have hugged him and said I was ready. This was in the days when the agricultural community was a regime in itself. The farms were family affairs, with the average size being about five or seven cows, while a big farm would have twenty cows and twenty hectares of land. The fields were small and separated by low hedges, ditches, and trees to the point that as you came out of Avranches and descended the hill towards the Mont St Michel you had the impression you were entering a forest, with the Mont on the horizon.

The vet was also a character in himself. He was a decent old boy and was the only son of a French army general, another millionaire on my list. He had no idea as to where or precisely when he was born because the exact location of a general was top secret at the time; and so on his birth certificate for date and place of birth there simply figured "31 December 1936, military base 1234" or something like that. He not only taught me all about cows, sheep, pigs, farmers and farmers' daughters (and I am not joking, he was a randy bastard), he also taught me to navigate. This was an essential part of his veterinary practice. On doing the rounds in the farms, once the details had been settled, we would sit down at the inevitable long table with benches either side in front of the perpetual fire burning in the west chimney with the old granny in the bed on the north side and, in summer when the door was left open, chickens wandering in and out to scratch for crumbs under the table, get down to the more lucrative side of his business, as if veterinary medicine did not pay enough. All the top surgeons in France were failed vets. They took the veterinary entrance exam as first option and when they fail that they took surgery as second option. He had a yacht tied up in Granville and on our time off we would go over to Jersey and stock up on duty-free cigarettes and spirits. My chronic seasickness vanished overnight. The rest of the week, after delivering calves, gouging out the rot from sheep's feet, castrating pigs and poisoning the nation's meat with hormones, we would present our cut price merchandise in the farms where it was more than welcome. The Channel Islands customs had the bad habit of tipping off their colleagues in France if they saw anything unusual, but an Englishman buying in bulk aroused no suspicion. They presumed I was from the mainland, so I was a godsend to the vet. One day it was Jersey and the next was Guernsey, so we were able to greatly increase our stock with very little risk of being noticed.

Once I had acquired sufficient expertise in the veterinary art I was sent out alone to poison the meat, the then most remunerative side of the veterinary trade. Meat poisoning is a fallacy totally fabricated by the press of the day, much the same as Françoise's Nazi babies. The routine was that in Normandy, milk production was the order of the day. The *Département of la Manche* was the prime milk producer of France but in order that a cow produces milk, she must first bear a calf. From the point of view of the farmer, the calf is a waste product. It's an ill wind which blows nobody any good; so secondary farmers bought up the calves, fattened them and sold them off as veal. Calves were sold live by the kilo, so the fatter the calf, the higher the profit. Our job was to fatten the calf in the quickest time possible and that involved castration. In order to avoid any unnecessary surgical suffering with the added risk of infection, and calves are unbelievably fragile things, the simplest solution was chemical castration and that implied the use of estradiol. The calf was separated from the mother at eight days and immediately given a primo dose of estradiol in the form of pellets under the skin. It then spent the following weeks in a stable, was given a booster dose at twelve weeks, before being sold to the slaughter house at fifteen weeks. No harm done anywhere. We would start at 5am and very often finish at 11pm and although we only charged the farmers 1 franc per dose, we were rolling in money. With the contraband added as a perk, we had no financial problems.

Personally, I am convinced the end of agriculture was a planned affair from the start. We started off with an epidemic of brucellosis, which greatly reduced the value of the stock and bankrupted many small farmers, immediately followed by an epidemic of foot and mouth disease, which I am certain was introduced on purpose. During three months all bleach products vanished from the shop shelves and it was impossible to buy things like Vim, Ajax, or Javel. When the epidemic was declared the army came down to give a hand and, just by miracle, they had an unlimited stock of bleaching powders and liquid. Once that was over, the brucellosis returned. All cows had to be tested so blood samples were sent off to the prefecture laboratory. If a cow was positive we would punch a hole the size of a 20p coin in one ear. After it had aborted, a second hole was put through the ear beside the first which ensured the cow could not be sold for anything other than what it was really worth, in other words, next to nothing because the cow would abort four years running after contracting the disease.

At the same time the government decided on a program of *"remembrement"*. This involved tearing up all the hedges and trees which bordered the small fields, flattening out the embankments and ditches, leaving giant fields of over five hectares separated only by interminable lines of barbed wire. On descending the hill from Avranches you no longer had the impression of entering a forest, but you had the creepy feeling you were passing through the badlands after a nuclear attack. Agriculture was on the way out. The "Common Agricultural Policy" had failed.

Nowadays the small farms have all gone, replaced by the big industrial affairs. Today, if a cow even looks as if something is wrong it is considered to be a waste of time and money treating it and is sent directly to the slaughter house. All the old vets from Normandy now work in the Paris region, treating rubbish like dogs, cats, goldfish and canaries. One vet found a job at Rungis market and complained to me that he spent all his life doing the farms only to become a meat *gendarme*, certifying carcases. One other poor guy returned to Normandy one night and blew his head off in a field.

One backfire effect of the job was that I never eat steak in Normandy any more, although I can presume things have changed since those days. Very often a cattle truck would pull up in the courtyard with a half-dead cow inside. Nine out of ten times this would be a spinal infection, which only declares itself after things are too late to do anything about it. When a cow lies down to chew the cud, very often another one will step on its tail provoking an infection which, eventually, reaches almost to the brain. The only thing the farmer wanted was a shot of adrenaline so the cow could remain alive for the journey to the nearest slaughter house and walk under its own steam on arrival. Otherwise it would be a job for the knackerman. That completely put me off bovine meat.

Things came to a sorry end when a law was passed banning the use of estradiol. There were seventeen vets in parliament, who all voted against the law; but the press assault overshadowed reason. Day after day there were stories in the papers of, "I bought a lump of veal and it shrivelled up to one square inch of meat in the frying pan" or, "I gave my son veal and he started growing breasts immediately afterwards", in much the same way as "Alsatian eats its dead owner" six years previously. The country vet had his days numbered! As a rough calculation you would need to eat the veal every day over a period of 20 years to obtain the same build-up of estradiol that a woman taking a contraceptive pill absorbs every month. So much for the press. This was followed by a law imposing quotas on milk production.

Veterinary medicine fell off overnight but on the road on the opposite side of Avranches, going towards Villedieu, there was an auberge called the "Belle Epoch" which looked as if its better days were over, although there were always lights inside during the evenings and at night. It once had been the very first discotheque in the region but now it looked closed except for a sign outside advertising "fast food" meals at 7.50 francs complete with wine. In those days nobody had ever heard of fast food so the sign meant nothing to the passers-by. I casually asked a few people in town about it and learnt it was once a thriving auberge complete with bar, restaurant, and disco, but the owner was now under the menace of closure for running a brothel. Wow! I just had to find out more, so on one return drive after putting Françoise on the train for Paris I called in.

The front door gave way directly into the bar reception and the restaurant was in a small room to the right at the far end of the long building. The waitress was a fairly heavy woman, several years older than me, called Marthe. I asked about the discotheque and she called the owner. Gerard was about my age and was what the French call a *"pied-noir"*, someone born in the north Sahara colonies, who had been obliged to drop everything and run, carrying only one suitcase, after the Algerian war of independence ended. He was also a homosexual, which further blackened his reputation as a brothel keeper.

He told me how, when he first acquired the building, it was a blacksmith's shop with an adjoining stable and hay loft above. He converted the shop into a kitchen, bar, and restaurant, built the disco in the stables, then fitted out six bedrooms and his own quarters in the loft. He gave me a guided tour, saying he had to refurnish the disco after the local authorities had declared it did not conform to the safety standards.

I knew a lot about discos because five years previously the Avranches vet, in a fit of madness, had left his cows to buy a discotheque in St-Germaine-en-Laye near Versailles. A fire somewhere in a discotheque in Grenoble on the Swiss border the following year had cost the lives of 146 persons, most of them youngsters, and the regulations changed drastically. The cost of modifying his building was not worth the effort so he sold up and returned to his cows. I told Gérard, if he wished, I could give a hand on the transformations during my spare time, and he agreed. On much the same basis as Françoise had hired me at Princedale Road back in 1966, Gérard said he could not afford to pay me anything but I could drink all the beer I wanted in return for doing the odd jobs. It was not long before he realised his mistake; but now I was fully occupied and having fun at the same time.

November 1975 saw Christiane's eighteenth birthday and her liberation from her grandmother's overpowering restrictions. She was free. But Christiane had one enormous natural defect: whereas like most schemers Françoise had a certain degree of intelligence in her favour, Christiane was hopelessly thick and stupid. Six weeks after her eighteenth birthday she arrived with Françoise at the presbytery to spend the pagan "Winter Solstice" together. This was when I discovered the lesbian relationship between them.

I was permitted to sleep in the guest room upstairs while they were together and the only reason my presence was tolerated at all was because of my distant Transylvanian blood.

At eighteen, and hardly able to read and write, Christiane was running the household like a five year old child carrying a gun. Françoise had come up with the good idea of marrying her daughter off to her cousin Olivier, the son of Robert-Henri's brother Jean. Olivier had no idea as to what was going on behind his back, while Françoise was plotting the splendid marriage between Christiane de Caumont la Force and Olivier de Caumont la Force.

Françoise contacted her old friend Jacques de Ricaumont at the *Association de Noblesse* with the intention of making Christiane a prominent member, and her application was accepted. Although I had never met him, I felt really sorry for the future groom. During the brief visits in the company of her grandmother, Christiane had remained fairly discreet, but now she had been freed of her chains she began to show her true nature. She must have been one of the most perverted and degenerate creatures I have ever come across in my entire lifetime.

A few years ago on the Internet I read a post by one guy who was evidently turned on by the thought of lesbianism and asked everyone if they had any ideas as to how he might persuade his wife to give it a try. In less than twenty-four hours he had received over two hundred replies all saying, "Whatever you do, don't try it!" The reason given was that he would suddenly find himself to be a useless accessory and, in all probability, booted out of his own home before very long. His correspondents knew exactly what they were talking about; this was precisely the situation which developed in the presbytery on Christiane's arrival.

I never had any problems with Françoise, she was born and bred bisexual. But, for Christiane, Ducey was an entirely new life compared to the one to which she had been accustomed. She now considered herself to be the new mistress of the house and I was the accessory. Françoise, in her delusion about the future marriage and the renaissance of her court at Maxim's, was totally blinded to the reality of the situation and Christiane made everything turn to her advantage in her attempts to poison her mother's mind against me; in exactly the same way as Betty had alienated her from the few people capable of protecting her from herself while she was in Holloway. Concerning her intelligence, she could only be described as existentialist, the same as a cockroach; no brain but a highly developed central nervous system, which permitted her to exist in her immediate surroundings with no notion concerning anything to be found outside her immediate presence.

From morning to night, life at the presbytery during the holiday was nothing but Christiane's marriage and Hungarian rhapsody. Christiane began to outwardly despise me and only on several rare occasions did Françoise weakly support me. Christiane was in total control. Finally, the only thing which prevented me from bringing Christiane's short life to term was when they returned to Paris after New Year was over. After they had left I painted my own version of an old IRA slogan on a wall in the garage beside the cider press. It read, "Rem.X.75", remember Xmas 1975. It served as a continual reminder that one day I would have the satisfaction of watching Christiane suffer in the same way as my own life had been a sheer misery during that winter solstice.

Each evening after the sun had set I lit a black candle under the inscription inviting the Divine Justice to exact a just revenge. Divine Justice is a reality which I learnt to respect long before I had left Britain. As a child it frightened me, but with the passage of time it became a reassuring friend. You rarely have to call upon its intervention. Divine Justice operates following its own rules, in its own time limits; and always unexpectedly.

Although they returned to Ducey only at spaced intervals, for the rest of the time I was tranquil and well occupied with the farm animals, the disco under construction, and moonfleeting between the Channel Islands and Granville. The year wore on slowly but I was kept more than busy. One icy cold day, with a fair layer of snow on the roads, I was passing through a village when I noticed an isolated house on a corner with the customary yellow post box on the wall by the door and a publicity sign over one window advertising my favourite beer. I decided to stop. I mounted the few steps of the only door which gave onto the road with no pavement and entered a large comfortably warm and welcoming room. There was a long table set out by the far wall with about a dozen or so people enjoying a midday meal and, as I could not see the counter of the bar, I settled down at one table in a corner by the door near an open fire. Everyone stopped eating to inspect the stranger. Villagers are more curious than cows concerning outsiders entering their field but finally one man left the table and approached me. I said good morning and asked for a beer. He looked surprised to see me but he went to a nearby refrigerator, took out my beer then returned to the long dining table to find me a glass. On his return I asked the price, gave him a few coins with the customary tip added and thanked him. He went back to his place at the long table and everyone returned to their meal.

After I had finished my beer and warmed up beside the fire I rose, politely said goodbye to everyone and left. As I was driving away, I realised to my horror the building was not a bar at all but a private house. The post box and publicity sign were on the walls simply for strategic reasons and I had burst in on a family meal.

The brucellosis kept everyone busy and one day, after visiting a farm, I turned to the vet and said that we had forgotten to wash our boots before leaving. If the next farm was clean on our arrival it would be contaminated before we left. He shrugged and said at least we had some more work guaranteed. A few days later we brought the lab results to one farmer who had already tied his six cows to a fence in a row in front of the stable awaiting our visit. I made myself comfortable between the cows while the vet pulled out the results sheet. I read out the number on the first cow's plastic identity tag which is clipped into its ear at birth.

"12345AB."

"Positive," came the reply. So I pulled out my punch and made a hole in the ear just under the tag.

"Whuuuuu." What the hell was that? It sounded like a banshee. We both looked at each other in amazement. I gave the cow's ear a pull then jabbed it in the ribs with the handle of my punch. No further sound came so I moved on to the next cow.

"44556CD."

"Positive." And I made the reglementary hole.

"Whuuuuu." The banshee had returned. I pulled this cow's ear to no avail and we began grinning at each other.

"88811JK."

"Positive."

"Whuuuuu." I could not stand it any longer and started laughing. Neither of us had ever heard a cow make such a strange noise.

"90101ZA"

"Negative." No hole, no banshee.

"65432GF."

"Positive."

"Whuuuuu."

We were both nearly doubled up with laughter. The next cow was negative but four out of six was not a bad score. By the time we left the row we both had tears rolling down our cheeks.

We clung on to each other and sought out the farmer, when, all of a sudden, we heard the curious "Whuuuu", coming from inside the stable. The farmer was sitting on a milking stool crying his eyes out; while we had been laughing like a pair of fatuous comedians clipping his herd into worthlessness. We handed him the results sheet then made a bolt for the car before he decided to get his shotgun and blow his head off, probably beginning with ours.

One day while out with the hormones I had a student with me. Sometimes the calves are all herded together in a giant stable and catching them one by one for the implant can be harder work than in a rodeo, but the great majority were kept in small individual stalls in a row. This is a job for two; one goes behind to push the calf forward, while the other does the implant in front. Once I was pushing when the calf backed up suddenly and I slipped off the planks, falling into the trench of liquid manure behind me. I was covered from head to foot. I let the student go behind, at the same time giving him his instructions. The dose of estradiol is different for a male or a female, so the pellets are kept in either one pocket or the other in the blouse. He pushed the first calf forward and I waited. Finally I asked,

"Male or female?"

No reply.

"Is it a boy or a girl?"

Still no reply. Finally a weak voice from behind the row asked,

"How can you tell?"

Jesus Christ! How on earth did he pass his entrance exam? In all, I could write a book about veterinary life in the Normandy countryside during the seventies and I was sorry when French agriculture finally died.

It was while doing the farms I had my first introduction to rural political life. There were two extremist movements at the time: the Mouvement Normand, a Normandy separatist movement which had grown up in the history department of Caen University and consisted mostly of intellectuals; and the FLB, the Front for the Liberation of Brittany who were out and out bomb-chuckers, along the same lines as the IRA, except the Bretons were Nazis.

I ran into one guy, Joël Tropée, who I can only describe as a bigger crook than Jean-Louis Bernard. They were in the same trade. They even physically resembled each other. Joël lived in two luxury caravans in the corner of one of his mother's fields and drove a Cadillac. He started off as a carpet salesman, but you do not drive a car like that selling carpets in farms with beaten earth floors and chickens wandering about under the table. As part of his sales pitch he had the good idea of starting to tell fortunes to entertain his clients; a few cards on the tables and a bit of palmistry, and discovered he could make more money predicting the future to an already superstitious simple-minded rural community than by selling Persian rugs. He kept his salesman's status simply for tax purposes. He was born in Brittany but lived just over the border in St James in Normandy, near the American war cemetery. At some time during his carpet career he ran foul of a Jewish enterprise, so it came of no surprise that he eventually found himself in contact with the FLB. From there he progressed to the MN.

By the time I met him he dressed entirely in white with a gold chain about his neck like one of the modern day self-styled Druids which abound and flourish in Brittany like Holy Messiahs in Jerusalem at the time of Pilate. Just like the Messiahs they are two a penny and you can find one on any street corner. To gain publicity he hit on the idea of standing as candidate for the MN in the elections for the Conseil Général, the equivalent of a county council election. He stood no chance of being elected. In rural communities the councillors were always ether the local doctor, the local lawyer or the local vet; it was simply the publicity he was after. Like Tixie, he did manage to win 5% of the vote and keep his deposit. What I did not realise was that he had the RG on his back until one day he was carted off to St Malo prison where he spent six months in *"prevention"*, a curious French legal technicality where you can spend years behind bars without a trial while the Juge d'Instruction carries out an investigation.

I once read a very interesting article by the journalist Fenton Bresler, entitled, "Britain doesn't need this frightening judge," where he explains, although the Juge d'Instruction is the most minor figure in the French judicial hierarchy, paradoxically, he is also the most powerful. I knew exactly what Joël was up against. The charges against him were that he was giving his children an SS education, whatever that might be, and that he practiced black magic with them - because his children were suffering from monkey bites. Considering Joël did not own a monkey I thought this was all a bit far-fetched. After six months in St Malo his father in law confessed that some unknown figures had menaced him into making the accusations against him. This might have been the work of the RG but, whoever was to blame, his fortune telling days were over. He decided to start up a world- wide mail order sect called *"Eglise christique de la Jerusalem nouvelle – Ordre de Raolf, d'Arnold et d'Osmond"*, based at St James and, working along the same lines at the Rosicrucians in San Jose, California, contacting his adepts by mail.

What with my own problems with Christiane and Françoise, which were to worsen as time went on, I lost touch with Joël. But not before he introduced me to many interesting personages on the separatist scene in both Brittany and Normandy. When I did eventually catch up with him towards the middle of the 1990's, he was destitute, living in the Red Cross hostel for the homeless in Caen. By then I was living in Evry.

His tale was horrific. As a mail order sect he enjoyed a great success, eventually earning enough money to be able to create four limited companies, in Madagascar of all places. Everything was done on a humanitarian basis, which included the importation of medicines to alleviate what had become one of the poorest populations of the world; a veritable clairvoyant Harry Lime. His mentor was none other than Albert Zafy, who held the presidency for three short years, beginning in 1993, lasting until 1996. Zafy was born in Madagascar but had been to university in Montpellier and Paris, eventually becoming a professor of surgery. He became the Malgache Minister of Health under General Ramenantsoa, returning to medicine at the University of Madagascar in 1975. Joel managed to sink his hooks into Zafy, becoming his councillor by the bias of Zafy's wife who is quoted as saying, "He (Zafy) is stubborn; let's hope he listens to you."

From then on Joël saw himself as an African Rasputin with a black Tsarina to please. He had the president's ear and could do no wrong, at the same time making enemies all the way down the road. Things came to a sorry end the day Zafy was booted out of power. Joël and his family were booted out of Madagascar the following day. In all he lost about ten million French francs, six and a half million of which vanished without trace from his account in a French bank in Antananarivo. As a final gesture of appreciation for services rendered they gave Rasputin a mock firing squad in front of his family in the grounds of his villa just before he left, just to discourage him from ever thinking of returning one day. The joke on Joël is on their deportation orders. The family is described as "of Jewish origin."

The last I heard of him was that a once respected member of the Order of Chartered Accountants in Nice was up in arms against Joël for swindling him up to the point where he was struck off the Order. Today he practices ethno-medicine on the Mediterranean coast.

CHAPTER 19

Lesbian bed death

One day, late in the autumn of 1976, Françoise and Christiane arrived at Ducey, but instead of the usual mutual adoration, they were hostile and continually quarrelling. Most surprising of all, Christiane no longer had her long hair down to her waist but had been cropped short, in the style of a boy. Her dresses had given way to a pair of blue jeans and her breasts had been artificially flattened out with bandages. The reason was simple. Over a period of twenty years too much had changed in Paris. Maxim's was finished as the centre of social life and Françoise now held her small court in another lesser known landmark, the Cintra, a bar immediately opposite her mother's building in the square built by her grandfather.

Once upon a time this chic bar and restaurant in the secluded square had seen much of the artistic life of Paris, including frequentations by Sidonie-Gabrielle Collette where she wrote the greater part of her book *Gigi* at her favourite table in one corner, and the actor Louis Jouvet who always played in the Athenée theatre, next door to the bar. Now the decline which had hit Maxim's was everywhere and the Cintra was operated by a coarse woman named Renée from Marseille, who would have probably been better off running a bar for seamen in her native Mediterranean port. Renée had immediately realised the potential to be found in Françoise; and at once set her ambition on fleecing Françoise in exactly the same way as so many other entrepreneurs had done in the past. The greater part of the Cintra's evening clientele now consisted, not of the high class theatre-goers of the past, but of union bosses from the Atlantic ports, up to town on their members' funds; and police from the Paris anti-gang brigade.

As Coco Chanel once said, "Any publicity, even bad publicity, is better than no publicity at all." So it was for Françoise, any attention was better than no attention at all. She was not unhappy though. This life was a far cry from her aristocratic castles but it did resemble the kitchen table in the basement of the Nazi headquarters back in London where she had plotted in the past. Only one thing spoiled the effect. In spite of aesthetic surgery and expensive clothes, she was now 44 with an 18 year old beautiful daughter at her side. Even if she was thick and stupid with no valid conversation, Christiane was attracting far too much attention and Françoise was beginning to play second fiddle.

By now even Françoise could see the days of the fifties were over. The carefully planned and plotted marriage between the two cousins would achieve very little, and, in any case, her first husband, Robert-Henri, had already remarried back in 1969, with a Polish aristocrat and would hardly be pleased to see his "ex" anywhere near the family *château* at Fontaine-Française again. On the other hand, the lads from the anti-gang were a cheerful enough crew with their stories of a clandestine life and muscular arrests.

They all carried guns and didn't hesitate to use them, sometimes even shooting each other by mistake, which is the origin of the scarlet armbands which the police wear today when sudden action is called upon. At the flash of a card they were totally exempt from the law; they tortured their prisoners up to the point where most countries in the world now refuse extradition towards France and suspected terrorists prefer to live abroad. Their "friends" enjoyed extraordinary privileges over ordinary citizens and so, in general, Françoise had found a modern day SS, even if they were republican and hardly likely to burn down Dior's boutique in the avenue Montaigne, something which Françoise had more or less forgotten during her enthusiasm for everything Hungarian.

She was not going to let Christiane steal her limelight and the remedy was to make her as hideous as possible. She played on the lesbian aspect of her daughter's psyche. But instead of enhancing her beauty, the same beauty which she herself had at first admired, she worked on the darker side of sapphism. Christiane was to become the perfect "butch", which would prevent her from eclipsing her mother. Hence the cropped hair, the masculine style of dress, bandages around the breasts instead of a bra; and even a change of name. Françoise asked me if I could come up with any ideas for a symbolic name and I did. Immediately opposite Maxim's in the rue Royale is a clothes shop called "Fred". From now on Christiane became "Fred".

Normally during their visits Françoise always managed to find a few moments when we could be alone and I could satisfy her in the way I had so often done in the past. So it came as a thunderbolt when all of a sudden she took both me and Christiane into the bedroom and started to undress her daughter in exactly the same way as she had undressed so many women from Avranches. Who was I to refuse? This now became our normal routine whenever they came to Ducey.

Right from the very start I never believed for one minute that Françoise, with her dominant character, would let Christiane call the tune for very long. But now, no matter where Françoise went, "Fred" clung to her side in an appalling dog like devotion; and no matter what curious spectacle "Fred" represented, Françoise's age, heavy drinking and chain smoking were beginning to take their toll. Christiane, strange as she appeared, was still the centre of attention and this was too much for Françoise. She visited Ducey, where she had been happy, more and more frequently and we spent a lot of our time in the Belle Epoque, where "Fred" had found a great friend in Gérard. Very often we would leave her there and return to the presbytery together, but all the time I had the impression something was bothering Françoise's spirit. I asked what was wrong and under normal circumstances she would have opened her heart to me, but she simply sat there, looking at the wall, avoiding my eyes. The unlimited cash appeared to have run out. She must have squandered the revenue from my book, something of which I was oblivious at the time. But lack of cash had never been a problem in the past. We were used to living on credit.

Another radical change had taken place with the passage of time. Françoise's adoration of the pagan Nordic gods had slowly degenerated into what can only be described as devil worship. Borisz had given her an old photograph of her father dating back to the days when he had a monastic inclination. He was sitting at his desk reading a book with a candle and a skull on the table beside him, the two symbols which, along with digging a few inches of their own graves every day, remind the monks that their days on earth are numbered. Very often they also have a small inscription on the same table taken from

Matthew, 24.42, "Watch therefore, for ye know what hour your Lord doth come". Few people outside mysticism understand the true significance of this phrase and it would have been a waste of time trying to explain it to Françoise. She copied her father but added a more sinister tone. We went to a cemetery near Granville where she collected a few bones, including a skull, from the common grave, which she placed on the altar of her chapel. From then on her disposition towards the macabre slowly took over.

Several years earlier, I had painted Christiane's leopard coat of arms on an oak tablet which she had hung up on the wall over her bedroom door at the apartment in Paris. Now she wanted some satanic arms to replace them. I copied something out of one of my *Man, Myth, and Magic* magazines, which seemed to please her. It consisted of a blazon depicting a salamander in a fire, with a lion rampant either side, one surmounted with an inversed pentacle, the sign of the Devil. At the same time, she bought two silver crosses from the shop at Notre Dame in Paris and asked a jeweller to pierce a hole at the lower end, so that both she and Françoise could wear the inverted crosses on a chain about their necks. Christiane also wore a green butterfly broach, the animal undergoing the greatest metamorphosis in the animal world, which in Catholicism symbolises the souls of the dead waiting to pass through purgatory. By wearing it in an inversed position, for her it symbolised the passage through the infernal realms.

Both Françoise and Christiane refused to understand that Satanism, exactly the same as cocaine or alcoholism, once the habit has taken root, it is impossible to find a way out. The only remedy is to have never started, as from the beginning. It lives with you for the rest of your life. Any former addict will confirm, "You can forget the coke, but the coke won't forget you." Any reformed drinker knows that one single glass will summon up the others. A pact with Satan will have to be honoured one day. Something which began as a game for Françoise and Christiane was to end in tragedy for both of them, but, in 1976, the amusement had only just begun. In reality very nearly all the organised satanic cults, churches, or sects are nothing more than either an elaborate game or a lucrative money-raking racket. Few people realise the Luciferian cult, real or imaginary, is a very serious affair; with grave consequences awaiting those who are not sufficiently versed in the mystical arts.

The essence of Satanism is evil and it is next to impossible for any mortal to perform an evil act. The true notion of evil has nothing to do with any community or religious written code but is strictly personal. What may be evil for one person would have no evil context for another. To a lesser degree, collectively it is evil in Islam or Judaism to eat pork; whereas, for many people the world over, pork as a cheap meat goes to make up part of the basic alimentation. Pork is nothing more than a question of collective opinion.

On a more serious personal scale, you could give a gun to two different persons with the instruction to shoot their mother. To someone who hates their parent to an extreme degree, this would not seem evil. The only deterrent being the obligation to face criminal justice afterwards, where the act would be considered evil on a collective basis. For someone who deeply loved their parent the act would be evil, and impossible to achieve.

Françoise and Christiane overlooked the finer details and set about their new hobby with enthusiasm. Their new master was the Devil to whom they swore allegiance. They made the same mistake, exactly as did so many volunteers for the French Charlemagne division of the SS during the war, believing their new master would honour them with extraordinary powers and graces beyond the reach of ordinary mortals. Evidently the "Collabos" had never read the passage in Mein Kampf which clearly states that National Socialism is not a product for exportation. In the eyes of the Nazis they were nothing more than foreign cannon fodder. The situation is exactly the same with the Devil, he does not rely on helpers; his only aim is to destroy the creature created in God's image. If the creatures voluntarily submit to their proper destruction without all the bother of being obliged to tempt them, all the better, but they need not think they will be rewarded for their stupidity.

To add to the fun, Christiane managed to take a Book of Common Prayer from the English church of St George in Paris. In the evenings she would lay naked on the dining room table with a collection of candles, mirrors and other diverse trappings placed around her body, while I read a satanic version of the Holy Communion. The triangle had been completed. Needless to say, as with nearly all the diverse devil worshipping cults and churches worldwide, everything ended in bed afterwards. Which, for many Satanists, is generally the object of the exercise to begin with.

In the domain of higher mysticism all religion suddenly becomes superfluous and future development takes on an austere personal obligation to continue alone. This does not mean devoid of any external assistance. The Bible alone is overflowing with instructions for those who understand their hidden meaning, but this is far beyond the comprehension of the Catholics or Protestants in the street who are prepared to throw nail bombs at each other in the name of their varying interpretations of a text, or Shiites and Sunnis killing each other because they believe Mohammad wanted something done in one specific way and not another. If Christiane and Françoise had found a new distraction I was prepared to keep them happy.

This situation continued for nearly a year, although their visits to Ducey became more and more infrequent. I had more than enough to keep me busy. But finally, during one visit, Françoise asked me to leave Ducey and come to live near Paris in her mother's *fermette* at Noisy-sur-École in the district of Fontainebleau. I could not quite see the reasoning behind her request. But after we had ironed out all the details we fixed the moving day as the first of August, 1977.

CHAPTER 20

Noisy-sur-École and Milly-la-Forêt

During the weeks that followed our arrangement I travelled several times between Ducey, Paris and the village of Noisy-sur-École, preparing for the day of the great transfer. On the Monday morning in question, after giving the last of the dogs its sleeping shot, I loaded them into the van, which one of Gérard's friends had proposed to drive, and we set out on the three hundred and thirty kilometre trip to the *fermette*. I lost the van at some traffic lights in Alençon and, after having taken different directions, we finally met up again at the *fermette*.

Evening was setting in. Once everything had been unloaded we went out looking for something to eat. I had the impression I had left Normandy to settle down in the middle of nowhere. We discovered there was nothing at all in the village of Noisy, not one single shop or bar, and the nearest café in Auvers was closed on Mondays. The next town along the road was Milly-la-Forêt and everything was closed there too. I was beginning to wonder into exactly which hole I had fallen. We found the only café open was in Fontainebleau, twelve miles away through the thick forest.

I spent the rest of the week settling in and exploring the surrounding countryside. For a millionaire's secondary residence the *fermette* could best be described as a ruin. On my first night I received a violent electric shock as I switched on the light in my bedroom. The wiring dated back to well before the war and was probably the original circuit when Madeleine had bought it. A local electrician came to have a look and offered to rewire the whole house, but Madeleine found the estimate too expensive so I was reduced to switching everything on and off with a pencil.

There was a small courtyard in front of the house with two stables where I housed the dogs. Behind the house was a large garden and finally a field of one hectare adjoining that. Behind the stable on the hill side we had six hectares of forest for the dogs. When I first arrived it was six hectares of virgin jungle. To avoid costs the gardener had received orders to limit his activities to the garden alone. In 1977, Madeleine had a monthly revenue of £8,000, while an average week's wage for a production worker at IBM in Corbeil-Essonnes was £20.

She was such a miser she made Scrooge look like a spendthrift. Her Peugeot 404 was thirteen years old and when it was time to change the spark plugs she kept on about the cost all day long as if it was my fault they had worn out and I ought to pay for them myself. On arrival from Paris each Saturday afternoon we always stopped at Milly for some groceries. I accompanied Madeleine into the superette where, week after week, she always bought exactly the same can of mackerel and the same bottle of cheap table wine amongst other articles. With every single item she would turn it over in her hands as if it was the first time in her life she had set eyes on it, before scrutinising the price to see if it had increased since the previous weekend.

I could see I was going to enjoy myself here and I

immediately began to regret my cow sheds and the Belle Époque. At least the Auberge d'Auvers Galant near Noisy was still open and the proprietor was a fellow fan of Pink Floyd.

On my arrival at Noisy, Françoise immediately put an end to my relationship with Christiane. Notwithstanding the unquenchable hatred I felt for the girl and which had never left me since the hell on earth she put me through when she had spent the winter solstice in Ducey, Françoise sensed Christiane was growing far too fond of me; and the relationship risked posing another direct threat to her already unstable position as the queen of her private court. Apart from trips to Fontainebleau, where they visited the hairdresser and did some shopping, or at mealtimes, Christiane was either confined to her room or permitted to sit in the garden behind the house.

Madeleine's apartment in Paris was no better than the *fermette*. Normally it should have been a sixth floor luxury flat but for me there was not much difference between Paris and Noisy. The only reason she put up with my presence was because she was making a savings by not having to pay Pierre to drive her about while she was in Noisy. She did not have to bring Sadia the cook with her for the weekend, it was me and Françoise who prepared her meals, and I could start clearing the jungle if I wanted the dogs to have somewhere to take their exercise.

On my first weekend in Noisy she decided one of her old dresses needed to be repaired in order to avoid buying a new one and at the same time Françoise wanted a new evening gown cut for one of her evenings in a *tzigane* nightclub. So I was sent off to Milly la Forêt to collect the dressmaker who attended their needs. The *couturière* in question already had several millionaire clients, including Isabelle, the wife of the

French pop singer Claude François, and the aging Paulette, the proprietor of one of the manors in Milly who was just as, if not more miserly than Madeleine. This one lived in only one room of her gigantic manor and went so far as to wear dresses made from her dead husband's trousers. I found the *couturière's* address and when she opened the door I felt exactly the same shock as when I first stood before Forte's mistress in Coventry.

Sylvie was the eighth out of nine children of a Belgian stonecutter who had come to live in France between the wars. I immediately thought of my cathedrals and of asking him to reveal some of the secrets of his work, which still puzzled me, but he had died five years earlier of silicosis, the miner's disease where the lungs gradually fill with granite dust. While I was driving Sylvie to Noisy she told me she was in instance of divorce and I made up my mind on the spot that I would marry her. Strictly by coincidence we were both born in 1946.

After that weekend my main preoccupation was to find different pretexts to see Sylvie. Everyone in Milly knew her and her family; it is a small town and one of her brothers owned a garage, another a car breaker's yard, and another did something in local herb agriculture. In all she had six older brothers, with one living in Belgium as did her older sister. Her younger sister was 100% handicapped with Down's syndrome and lived with their mother four kilometres away in Moigny-sur-Ecole. Milly is a world famous centre for aromatic herb production, especially renowned for its mint. Jean Cocteau is buried in the Chapel of St Blaise, the fourth century doctor and auxiliary saint who became famous for his healing powers. His *"simples",* medicinal herbs, grow in the grounds around his chapel. Cocteau renovated the chapel soon after he had bought the *château* of Milly.

The town itself is extremely rich in history, from being the birthplace of St Wulfram, archbishop of Sens, in 640, destroyed by the English in the 14th century, a walled town on the principal route between Paris and Lyon until the 18th century when the RN.7 became the main axis, slowly losing its prestige and walls, until the middle of the 20th century when it became a fashionable venue for Parisians and artists, including Jean Cocteau and Christian Dior. The Italian *couturière* Nina Ricci lived in the manor of Moigny, a few hundred yards further along in the same road as Dior.

Sylvie was born immediately opposite the chapel and now says that Cocteau is buried in what used to be their toilets when they were children. To pass the evenings I had signed on for some first aid courses organised by the local fire brigade, so I asked if she would like to join me. To my consternation, she said she already had the state and the Red Cross diplomas but, as soon as I qualified for mine, I asked if she would like to take the advanced speciality in reanimation, which she accepted. She complained afterwards that, instead of taking her out to the cinema in the evenings, I took her to Fontainebleau hospital where Dr Crispin, the surgeon in the emergency unit, gave his lessons.

Sylvie had just passed her driving test and one weekend, when Madeleine wanted something in Milly, I let Sylvie drive back to Noisy. She put the car in gear and backed straight into a wall. Madeleine said that between us we would smash her car to bits. I had done exactly the same manoeuvre when I had first taken the wheel. The reverse gear in a 404 was in the same position as occupied by the first in any normal car. The service station on the road to Fontainebleau where I always filled up also had a bar and I proudly figured amongst their top three customers. So at New Year, when we organised a midday meal of oysters and wine for the regulars, I took Sylvie along. There were about twenty of us in all but by evening very few of the banqueters could walk straight. I was fortunate that Sylvie could drive and when I woke up in the middle of the night wondering where I was she was fast asleep in bed beside me. A new phase of my life had begun.

Françoise hated her and on several occasions there would have been a cat fight if it had not been for the presence of Madeleine, who was much attached to her and permitted her to sleep at the *fermette* while she was away in Paris. At one point she even warned Sylvie not to approach Françoise because she was dangerous. Sometimes she annoyed Madeleine. In one room was a period sofa which Napoleon was supposed to have sat on while writing the speech which he delivered to his troops in the Cour des Adieux of the *Château* of Fontainebleau before being carted off to Elba. Sylvie tried it out and went clean through the cushions to the floor. Madeleine was far too tight fisted to pay to have anything treated for woodworm. The only thing which saved the situation was Maria, one of the maids. She had taken a monkey skin which served as a rug in the sitting room out onto the lawn and was thrashing it as if she wanted it to run away and climb a tree. Madeleine forgot about the sofa and dashed out into the garden to save the monkey's life. All this time Françoise was too busy chain smoking and preparing for her evenings out at the Tsarevitch in Paris. While Christiane could only stand by watching.

The Tsarevitch, in the rue des Colonels Renard behind the Arc de Triomph, was Françoise's favourite nightly haunt and sometimes I would accompany her. It was there I first met Tania who was a real live Russian princess. Tania Maximova-

Ivanov Princess Sviatopolsk-Mirski was short and tubby, exactly the same as Ninette, and was one of the last real "ladies of the night." She wore a wig but no underwear. For 500 francs, which she said she sent to London to aid her sister who lived in Britain, she would let you accompany her back to Levallois-Perret in the north Paris suburb where she lived. She must have been well into her eighties when I first met her and she was still lovely and full of charm. On the occasions when Sylvie came to the Tsarevitch, Tania would sit in one corner glaring at her. Françoise was worse than jealous of Tania, so my evenings at the Tsarevitch came to an end and she did not miss the opportunity to make certain Sylvie knew all about Tania. So one day, when I received a postcard, unfortunately signed "your little Tania" and asking me why I had not been to the nightclub recently, Sylvie immediately ripped it to shreds.

Sylvie's only real rival amongst the *tzigane* community was Marika and I adored her. Five years after Django Reinhardt had initiated his unique style of music in Paris, the Hungarian, Yoska Nemeth, began to appear at the Raspoutine in the rue Bassano. He became the undisputed prince of the *tzigane* musicians, while his wife Marika danced. Django Reinhardt died in 1953, aged only 42, and Yoska died twelve years later at the equally early age of only 44. When I met Marika she was elderly and was far from being the beautiful gipsy girl dancing on the sleeves of the disks which her husband had recorded during the height of their success together. She was scratching a living by singing in an obscure cabaret called the "Jockey Club" somewhere off Montparnasse and we took to each other instantly. Exactly the same as with Tania, Françoise's uncontrollable jealousy put an end to my visits there but, unlike the Tsarevitch, where she continued to spend her evenings, the Jockey Club was put on her own black list. All the evening Christiane would sit in the cabarets without saying a single word. At one point a magician in the Monseigneur, another Russian club just off the place de Clichy in the rue d'Amsterdam, who was half way through his act, apologised to her for waking her up. The whole room burst out laughing.

The last straw which broke the camel's back was Zina. She was a 100% true gipsy from the Lovara tribe with long black hair and raucous voice. She was so short she did not even come up to my shoulder but made up for her size in energy. Her husband Gueorgui would play the guitar while Zena danced for a while before abandoning the rest of their act by sitting on my lap drinking my champagne; leaving Gueorgui to rend his wrath on his instrument, playing it so furiously the strings would snap one after the other. In the end he would be doing his best to sing while strumming only one string, at the same time scowling in all vehemence in our direction. Sometimes I half expected him to smash his guitar over my head when he had finished but the 10 franc note which Françoise always gave him calmed him down. Zina would then follow me down to the toilets where we would try to chat together in a mixture of my beginner's Russian and her broken German. All gipsies are renowned for their infidelity, men and women alike. Great-great-grandfather Isaac Gosden would have been at home here if it had not been for Françoise. Thanks to having met Zina I was forbidden upon pain of excommunication to ever set foot in any *tzigane* club again for the rest of my life. At least I still had the Auberge d'Auvers Galant back in Noisy for a late night drink before going to bed.

I frequently left Sylvie in charge of the dogs while I went down to Ducey, just to make sure everything was still in order. The routine was that I began by airing the presbytery before cutting the hedges and pruning anything which might have given the place an abandoned air. Then I carried out a routine verification of everything, starting with the kennel and finishing in the attic. One day I was just preparing to return to Noisy when a motor cycle appeared and a telegraph boy called at the door. The telegram was from Françoise and had been sent from the post office in the boulevard Haussmann behind the Opéra. It read, "Don't move. I'll be on the 9pm train at Villedieu."

CHAPTER 21

Delenda Christiane Est

Françoise had been growing more and more fed up with Christiane as every day passed but one day the crunch came in the most unexpected way. The previous night there had been a power cut in the electricity and the food prepared the preceding evening by Sadia had been spoiled. Instead of wasting time doing extra shopping, more likely instead of spending extra money, Madeleine had ordered her to do her best with whatever was left. A hasty midday meal was served but there was not much of it. Only one small piece of meat remained and Madeleine insisted that Christiane should eat it because at twenty years of age she was still a growing girl. Françoise threw down her knife and fork, stormed out of the dining room and took the first train to Normandy.

When she arrived she remained as silent as the grave, while the heavy storm which was lingering in the night air added to the oppressive atmosphere as we drove down to Ducey. Having no idea what was amiss I had already prepared the log fire and candles as decoration. So, once we were in the sitting room, I mixed up her favourite cocktail, a whisky-sour, and we sat down on the English sofa with a damp evening breeze blowing through the house while distant thunder rumbled over the Mont St Michel. The storms arrived directly from the Atlantic before being captured in the bay where, if they were low enough, they circled indefinitely, bouncing time and time again off the hill of Avranches before finally continuing their way along the Channel. The electricity in the village was likely to be cut off at any minute by the storm and it could have been romantic if Françoise had not broken down crying. She explained through her tears how her daughter was totally overshadowing her life and how her dream had become a nightmare.

No matter what hideous aspect Christiane, or rather "Fred", now presented she was always twenty-five years younger than her mother. Chain smoking, alcohol and a failed aesthetic operation were taking their toll on Françoise. She was losing her court and was no longer the centre of attraction which, until now, had always been her principal interest throughout her life. I fathomed out the situation perfectly and immediately understood that somehow "Fred" had to be extracted from her daily animation, which was going to be a difficult job considering how Christiane had no special interest in life and spent all her waking hours following Françoise about like an energy sucking leech wherever she went.

After thirteen years in her company I knew Françoise perfectly and needed no explanation as to her frame of mind. I sensed she was going to ask me to bring Christiane to Ducey and keep her either here or at the Belle Epoque, giving Françoise the freedom to continue life without her presence in Paris. But I was more than surprised when she blurted out, "We've got to kill her!"

I just could not believe it. Less than two years previously Christiane was still a potential goddess, with her splendid marriage in view and, even though I had followed her rapid descent into the abyss with satisfaction, now she had suddenly become a potential corpse. I really hated Christiane but I thought the idea was somewhat extreme. If we had been in Paris or Noisy my reaction might have been different and I might have offered a more practical solution to Françoise's problem, saving Christiane from her mother's jealousy and wrath, but sitting here in Ducey and by closing my eyes I was able to relive every single moment of that winter solstice of 1975, and tears came to my own eyes, although my lament was not for the same reason as for Françoise. I went into the garage where my inscription, "Rem.X.75" awaited me. I lit what remained of a black candle on the makeshift shelf underneath the dust faded inscription on the wall, then returned to the log fire and Françoise.

We began the next day by following our usual routine, as if nothing had happened since the days when we lived in the presbytery together, with one exception, the dogs were in Noisy. The storm had cleared during the night and the sun had risen over a bright fresh day. We had a midday meal in a small café called the Grange de Tom on the route des Falaises at Champeaux, with its splendid view overlooking the bay of Mont St Michel, and there we discussed her plans over our working lunch.

The main preoccupation, which so many murderers overlook, was not how to go about the act, but the aftermath, that singularly neglected essential guaranteed to lead to arrest and condemnation in the courts. Which, in France, meant the guillotine. To plan a really good murder you must not start at the beginning and go forward but take things as from the end and work your way backwards.

She decided a cremation was imperative; no hope of an exhumation if things were to go wrong afterwards. In Britain all that is needed for a cremation are two doctors to give their opinion as to the cause of death; while in France things are more complicated, as the simplest things always are in this country. For an unnatural or sudden death the certificate has to be signed by a "médecin-expert" and it is the police who give the final decision concerning the disposal of the body.

Françoise was already familiar with the case of the British schoolboy who poisoned his classmates with cream buns laced with the rat poison thallium. Several years later a young technician in a photographic laboratory was accused of a similar crime. After a verdict of guilty had been achieved, it was revealed the schoolboy and the photographic technician were one and the same person. Thallium would have been the ideal vehicle for Christiane, the initial cause of death would be registered as by cause of gastro-enteritis, but she would be obliged to wait for the seasonal epidemic in the autumn where there are many deaths a day if that was to pass without being noticed.

The second choice was to slip an aconite root into her food or drink. Aconite, or monkshood, is undetectable unless the pathologist is expressly looking for it. The trouble was that the death of a young person, unless terminally ill or by cause of accident, is always suspect and the autopsy risked being detailed. Although some people cultivate it in their gardens, aconite grows wild, principally in the lower mountainous regions and although we could have found some in the Jardin des Plantes behind the natural history museum in Paris, it would be difficult to explain how Christiane came to ingest a lethal dose while living on the sixth floor in Paris, even though a sufficient dose is minimal in that introduction by means of a graze on the fingers while handling the product would be sufficient to bring about death. Françoise decided to return to Paris to think the matter over.

Inspiration came one only week later. One of Madeleine's tenants at the square had just been declared bankrupt and, unable to face the future, had taken the easy way out. He hanged himself. Being orthodox Jewish, which required burial in the shortest interval possible, he was dispatched in record time. She had completely overlooked suicide as a means of avoiding an autopsy so, sitting in Raymond Dior's favourite bar in the rue Caumartin, Françoise explained her macabre plan to me.

Relying on Christiane's unfathomable stupidity, her slavish unquestioning devotion to her mother, and the fact that she was totally incapable of thinking for herself, Françoise counted on enmeshing the girl into a sect-like indoctrination. She already partook to a minor degree in Françoise's new midday rituals, which had become diabolical, so she devised a whole series of initiatic rites based completely on a meaningless mumbo-jumbo which she had written especially for Christiane. Terminating with suicide as the liberating act which would be her passage into a higher transcendental plane where she would find her rightful glory and salvation. In other words, top herself and get out of Françoise's way as quickly as possible.

Using horoscopes and senseless out of context alchemic jargon the indoctrination process worked even quicker than first imagined. The date fixed for "Fred"'s transition was Wednesday, 21st June, the Summer Solstice 1978, a magical night.

Apart from standing at the end of a railway platform and

jumping in front of an express train, hanging is one of the suicidal methods with the lowest failure rate. With hanging, as with most suicides, they generally change their minds at the last minute. Once they have kicked the chair away they usually try to climb back up the rope. But by then it is too late. The police use the fact that their fingernails are torn out as one of the means of deciding whether the hanging was really a voluntary act or a murder in disguise. The only problem from her point of view was how to stay out of the affair. The solution was to feed Christiane enough spiel about the town of Lyon being the spiritual centre of France and that her transition must take place there. Françoise would obviously remain in Paris. While I was in Noisy, as usual.

On the Tuesday beforehand a small overnight bag was packed with the essentials for a short holiday inside. Although it was going to be a one way trip as far as Christiane was concerned there would be an enquiry afterwards and visitors arriving at hotels empty handed are always suspect clients. For the enquiry everything had to be perfectly normal. Christiane was so thick Françoise had to tie the knot for her in the nylon picture cord, the most suitable vehicle capable of taking her weight and being, at the same time, discreet enough to slip into her handbag. Christiane was put on a train for Lyon with a return ticket in her pocket for good measure at the enquiry and her head full of instructions on how to find a hotel as close to the centre of town as possible, test the bracket holding the curtain rail to the wall, then at midnight, kick the chair away.

Early next morning I received a phone call from Françoise. Christiane was so thick and stupid she had made a mess of the job and all she had achieved was a badly bruised neck and the bill to repair the curtain rail. We went to Lyon to collect her and settle the damages, but time was running out fast. After a failure like that even the stupidest dummy might begin to see through the plan; and so a second date was rapidly fixed. It was to be midnight after the 4th July, exactly two weeks later. The reason given to Christiane was that during the afternoon of Tuesday 4th July, the moon would be semi-sextile (30°) to Mercury in Cancer; which was a good enough reason considering her intelligence. Just to make certain nothing went wrong this time, Françoise fitted up the gallows herself.

Françoise had pushed Christiane out of her own bedroom in Madeleine's sixth floor flat, obliging the girl to sleep in one of the servants' rooms in the attic. It was a very small room, with just a bed, a wardrobe, table and chair, mirror and wash basin, a window which gave a limited view of the sky and surrounding roofing, and a wooden beam running across one corner by the door for taking coat hangers. She stood Christiane on the chair underneath the beam while the picture cord was adjusted with only enough slack to prevent her feet from touching the floor. The chair was left in position, the window was well secured from the inside to prevent any doubt as if it might have been a point of entry or exit from the room, then the rest of the morning was taken up with diverse incantations which Françoise invented on the spot to keep the evil spirits away. At midday the room was closed and they went down to the sixth floor to have lunch as if nothing out of the ordinary was happening. Life continued as normal.

All this time during the morning and afternoon I was in Noisy, where I had arranged for a close neighbour to take care of the dogs. Towards evening I drove back to Ducey with Sylvie. A few minutes before midnight we stopped off at a sportsmen's café in Alençon, aptly named so far as my attitude towards Christiane was concerned, "The Penalty". I stood Sylvie's little dog on the bar and made her do all her circus tricks which, although inherent in her nature, she had perfected over time with encouragement. She could walk about on her hind legs, roll about on her back and in all had a great success with the late night customers. So there would be no doubting as to our exact whereabouts at midnight on that fateful night.

As the night drew on Françoise took Christiane into the Cintra where they chatted with the usual lads from the anti-gang. At a quarter to midnight Christiane gave the excuse she was not feeling too well and returned to her servant's room, where the chair and picture cord were waiting for her. Immediately Françoise persuaded one of the police inspectors who later ambushed and gunned down the French gangster Mesrine in his car at the Porte de Clignancourt, to take her to a German bar on the other side of Paris. With an alibi like that she was as far out of the scene as I was, two hundred kilometres away in Alençon.

In the empty presbytery everything was dark and had an odour of humidity and abandon. I opened all the windows to change the stale air but after a recent storm the outside was just as damp as the interior. We had a quick night snack, while at the same time slipping Sylvie's dog into the bed to act as a warming pan. The long night drew on. Towards five o'clock the neighbourhood cockerels informed us morning had officially arrived, so we had breakfast, then set about arranging things as any other empty house needed arranging. I cut the overgrown hedges outside while Sylvie looked after the spiders' webs and dust. We were well occupied and, at midday, we decided to have a meal at a hotel in Pontaubault, the Paris-Brest.

Meanwhile, back in Paris, Françoise had woken up at

her usual time of ten-thirty, then taken her breakfast before carrying out her make-up ritual. After dressing she went into the Cintra for her first drink of the day and waited for Christiane to join her. At midday she expressed certain anguish to Renée concerning Christiane's inhabitual absence. Renée sent her son with Françoise to Christiane's room. There was no reply. So, after insisting and with a long pause without answer, the door was kicked in. Renée's son quickly turned Françoise around and took her downstairs. The coat hanger beam being immediately beside the door meant the poor fellow must have come face to face with Christiane on the end of her rope.

Towards one o'clock, at the end of our typically Norman lunch, I telephoned to Madeleine's Paris apartment from the Paris-Brest. The call was answered by one of the maids, Angelina, who was sobbing. She explained, between her tears, that mademoiselle Christiane was dead. I returned to the dining room and said to Sylvie, "Christiane est morte."

CHAPTER 22

The weeks and months which followed

We spent the remainder of the day closing things up at the presbytery, then returned to Paris, arriving at Noisy during the night. The next morning we went to the square to find Robert-Henri already in the sitting room with Madeleine and Françoise. By discretion we settled down in the small room which Madeleine used as her office. We could distinctly overhear everything which was going on in the sitting room and Robert-Henry, far from being the heartbroken father, was furious, cussing and cursing his nephew Olivier by every name under the sun.

According to his version of events, his daughter had hanged herself as a dejected fiancée, wantonly discarded by the love of her life, *cousin* Olivier. Knowing the exact truth of the entire situation, I had to laugh. Somehow, probably through gossip down at the *Association de Noblesse*, he had heard of the splendid marriage which was being plotted for the two cousins by Françoise. What he did not know was that Françoise had completely abandoned the idea at least a year previously, once she had realised the marriage would be completely useless concerning her own reintroduction into a waning Parisian social life, while at the same time she had begun to realise that the Countess Christiane was nothing more than a walking vegetable continually getting under her feet. As for the poor Count Olivier de Caumont la Force, I very much doubt if he ever had any knowledge of his splendid engagement with his cousin from the very start. Nothing could shake Robert-Henri's firm conviction that his daughter had unjustly died through a *"chagrin d'amour"*.

While he was still giving vent to his fury I decided to slip out for a quick beer. I went into the Cintra and could hardly believe my eyes; Renée was wearing Christiane's gold ring with her coat of arms on her own finger and was ostensibly flashing her hand about so that everyone present in the bar could see her acquisition. To add to the absurd spectacle she was wearing it on the wrong hand and in the wrong direction. When she noticed my presence I did not like the way she looked at me, because I could read her mind. Behind her scowl she was thinking, "From now on, I'm in control. If Christiane failed to get rid of you, don't think you'll be so lucky with me."

I could only smile looking at the ring and thought to myself, "There's a worse curse on that ring than ever there was on Alberich's Ring of the Nibelungen." I drank up my beer and then inwardly settled down to wait for the fun to begin.

Back in the apartment Robert-Henri was gone and that was the last I ever saw of him. Sylvie was comforting Madeleine while I went with Françoise to her bedroom to decide on our next course of action, at the same time giving her a severe warning against Renée in the Cintra. Upstairs the undertakers had laid Christiane out on a table and had covered her with a layer of carbonic snow. The clothes she had been wearing at the time of her death were neatly arranged in the wardrobe beside her; black underwear, a black pleated skirt, a black chemise and black shoes. She had followed her instructions to the letter.

There was a small indentation in the wooden coat hanger beam by the door where the picture cord had taken her weight. I took Françoise and Sylvie for a quick lunch in Raymond's favourite bar in the rue Caumartin. Then, leaving Françoise to play the part of a distraught mother, Sylvie and I returned to Noisy. My main preoccupation was now the impending game of chess about to be played against Renée. I decided to make the first move.

The *"médecin legiste"* had no difficulty in writing the death certificate. He put down, "strangulation by cause of *pendaison*." That was the end of the affair as far as he was concerned. The police *commissaire* of the 9e *arrondissement*, however, refused to sign the *"permission d'inhumation."* His instinct as an experienced police officer somehow made him doubt the entire scenario. He visited the apartment several times, where he "chatted," to use the technical term for an unofficial interrogation, with everyone in the household. About a week later, while I was in Milly, I was not surprised when I accidentally bumped into some old friends belonging to the RG from Normandy. We went into a bar on the market place where we discussed, amongst other things, Christiane's untimely death. When it came to the inevitable question of, "Where were you between 11pm on the 4th, and 1am on the 5th July?" they seemed genuinely disappointed when I gave the frank reply, "Alençon." They did not even bother to ask if I could back this up with anything but simply looked at each other, nodded, drank up and added before leaving, "We'll be seeing you later, maybe."

Life dragged on at Noisy; I only went to Paris once, to see

Françoise over some trivial details, and, after an interminable three weeks, the Commissariat reluctantly signed Christiane's inhumation certificate.

Only four persons were present for the cremation: Madeleine, Françoise, Gerard from the Belle Epoque, and myself. Robert-Henri must have had his own reasons for avoiding the ceremony. The hearse took Christiane's coffin and we followed in my car to the Columbarium at the Père Lachaise cemetery in the 20e *arrondissement*. In the large chapel Madeleine and Françoise sat in the front row, while I sat with Gerard behind them. At Christiane's own request it was a non-religious ceremony, but Madeleine had hired an organist who played throughout the waiting period between the coffin disappearing behind the curtains and the undertaker informing us the cremation had been completed. It was two and a half hours before he appeared.

The undertaker asked if we had anything which the deceased had asked to be placed in her *coffret* before it was sealed. She wanted to be committed to eternity with her inverted silver cross, which I had brought along in my pocket. But, at the last moment, Françoise turned around and slipped me her own inverted cross, asking me to add it at the same time. She now realised Devil worshipping was no game and wanted out. This was probably the reason she had rid herself of Christiane's ring so quickly.

The undertaker led me down to the crypt, which resembles more a system of tunnels, typical of so many of the small crypts under the churches of Paris which date back to the days when invasion was an everyday threat to the town. In one gallery the furnace was open. It can only be described as exactly the same as those used in the death camps which are on display today. The interior was glowing red hot and two of the undertakers were raking out the ashes. They were still giving off a humid vapour and an undertaker began to fill the casket with Christiane's remains, using a small trowel. The ashes continued to give off some steam and there were some pieces of rib poking out here and there which had not been entirely consumed by the fire. I dropped Françoise's cross into the casket, which was immediately sealed. I suppose the remainder of her ashes, which were still on the platform, finished up in some kind of a special dustbin reserved expressly for the surplus.

The undertakers then carried the casket up to where Madeleine, Françoise and Gerard were waiting to accompany Christiane to her final resting place in the Columbarium, while I followed with her inverted cross still in my pocket. If the curse on Renée's new ring was to bear fruit I would be needing some kind of a link between Christiane and her master, Satan.

I remained one more month at Noisy and, as the autumn approached, I decided to enact my first move in my game of chess with Renée. One of Sylvie's brothers had a large van so, just as in August 1977, the dogs were loaded up and I returned to Ducey in the company of Sylvie. Life in the presbytery was routine. The vet in Avranches was already preparing to fold up his practice and, all in all, Normandy was no longer the thriving duchy which I had left only one year previously. So much had changed in such a short space of time.

We dismantled Françoise's chapel. I used the candle sticks for different decorative purposes, placed her bone collection in a bag which I stored in the garage, and installed a television on the altar. Alsatian dogs have a very short lifespan and now there was no need to divide the survivors into two clans. With no gardener or cleaning lady a new aspect began to take over the presbytery. A severe drought in the summer of 1976 had already destroyed the greater part of the trees in the orchard, with the result that a bottle of cider which once had cost 1 franc in the farms was selling for 5 francs and a bottle of Calvados, which would have cost 10 francs, had totally disappeared from the circuit. At the same time a new law had been passed which prohibited anyone from carrying out their own distillation. The gigantic alembic on its cart drawn by a tractor which once had travelled from farm to farm had now become an exhibit in the agricultural museum.

To keep the grass under control I let a neighbour put some sheep and a couple of ponies in what was left of the orchard. Even Gerard was closing the Belle Epoque and was creating a limited company with his brother-in-law in Paris, dealing in kitchen equipment destined for large canteens and hotels. A stretch of the motorway which was one day going to link Paris to Brest via Caen had opened between Avranches and Pontorson, with the result that Pontaubault, which once required *gendarmes* to control the traffic flow during the weekends, now had shops closing one after the other as the tourists bypassed the town on the four lane express road. My Normandy was a thing of the past.

My only local distractions were a few of Joël Tropée's old friends in the FLB. But they were a dangerous alliance and I would have been better off avoiding their company. During the night of the 25-26th June, between Christiane's suicide attempts, the FLB had planted a bomb in the *"aile du Midi"* at the *Château de Versailles*, which caused an inestimable amount of damage to the national monument. This was the seventh bomb planted by the FLB that year.

The perpetrators were arrested within a few days, for the

simple reason that after the attack they assembled in a bar in the centre of the picturesque Breton town of Carhaix-Plouguer and were informing everyone at the tops of their voices how they had gone about their exploit. They forgot that one person in two in Brittany is a police informer. The perpetrators, who included Serge Rojinski of Russian origin, were sentenced to 15 years, but were amnestied by Francois Mitterrand when the socialist came to power in 1981. Rojinski taught the other prisoners Russian while he was serving his short sentence.

At the same time I met one of Rojinski's close friends named Bruno Renoult. Bruno's speciality involved trips to Moscow and other major Russian cities. It was the habit of the Red Army at the time to bury high ranking military officers in full uniform, complete with medals. Bruno scoured the Soviet press and when a sufficiently interesting officer died he would take a trip to Russia, dig up the deceased officer and sell his military regalia in one of the specialist shops around the place de la République in Paris.

Twenty-seven years later I would find myself standing next to Bruno at the *Tribunal de Grand Instance* of Saintes, on the Atlantic coast, accused of a million franc bank fraud. In reality the total figure was better than a win on the lottery but the court only took the singular figure into consideration because, at the end of the day, the banks were probably bigger crooks than us and, at the same time, the President of the Republic, Jacques Chirac, was under investigation himself for a fraud which made our figure seem pitiful, a fact that our third associate continually insisted upon in front of the *juge d'instruction*. After that episode Bruno finally lost his sense of adventure and today he is a respectable author, winning literary awards for his work in historical research.

Along with the FLB I also joined the *Mouvement Normand* where I met Georges Bernage. If the FLB were bomb chuckers, the MN were essentially intellectuals. Georges lived with his wife in a two-roomed apartment in the rue Royale in Bayeux and I was immediately struck by his resemblance to John Tyndall. He was living in dire straits and the good meal which he offered us consisted of a bowl of hot water with a lettuce leaf floating in it, a hot potato and one lump of bread. Although he had no cash, exactly the same as Tyndall, he was a shrewd businessman. He kept an old printing press in one corner of his bedroom and, like Tyndall, the party magazine *"Heimdall"* was registered in his personal name. Eventually his publishing house bore the name of "Heimdall Press." Sylvie felt sorry for the couple so she bought a pack of their overpriced Winter Solstice cards which we converted into Christmas cards.

When I saw him a few years later he owned the entire building. A secretary sneered at me and asked if I was a printer. I replied, "No, I'm his friend; or at least, I used to be." Publishing paid so well he moved out of Bayeux into the nearby countryside. I was surprised, when the 50th anniversary of the D-Day landing celebrations were televised in June 1994, to see at the very end of the credit titles, "......and special thanks to the historian, Georges Bernage."

The last time I called in to see him I was lost in the country lanes, so I asked a passing peasant (the *"paysan"* class still exists in France and is still a regime unto itself. It means "of the land"), where I could find Georges Bernage. He looked shocked and corrected me with, "MONSIEUR Bernage," and pointed to some trees. Above the treetops I could see the pinnacles of a large *château*. Georges had installed his office in the master's chambers on the first floor overlooking the grounds and when we entered the room Sylvie had a hard time to restrain her laughter. The guy who had once resembled Tyndall was now the twin of Jabba, the talking slug in Star Wars. He overflowed in his chair. To make matters worse, he told us that his wife had just left him for a lad only half her age. As it was, life between the FLB and the MN was a poor compensation for the Normandy I had known only one year previously.

One day while I was in Avranches I bumped into my two old friends from the RG who invited me for the customary beer. We were discussing the good old days when one of them suddenly came out with, "Your girlfriend has dual nationality. She has both French and Belgian passports." I was somewhat surprised and thought they were going to provoke some kind of trouble but they continued, "Your brother in law, the mechanic with the garage in Milly has got three cars registered with Belgian number plates." I could hardly see how her family came into this. Then they made a proposition, "How would you like to do a little job for us over the border? We can't do anything ourselves, we're French civil servants, but if you borrow one of your brother-in-law's cars, and travel with Sylvie, you should have no problems."

Then they added, "We'll make it worth your while and your expenses will be paid in full." I hardly needed to be asked twice so they gave me a rendezvous in Paris for two days later and some petrol vouchers which I could use in any Total service station in France. They were stamped on the back with, *"Ministère de l'Intérieur"* (The Home Office).

At the exact hour on the day in question I was standing on the steps of the Opéra when one of the officers came up to me. We went along to the metro at Havre-Caumartin and took a train to Miromesnil, two stops further down the line. From there we walked a short distance along the rue de Miromesnil to a café where two older colleagues whom I had never met before were waiting for us. I was introduced and the two others explained the details of what seemed to be an unbelievably well paid, simple job; and I wondered why they would ask me, of all people available, to carry out their task. I agreed to "give them a hand" without realising I was signing my own pact with a different devil to Françoise and Christiane.

In the meantime things were going badly for Françoise in Paris. Everyone I knew, including the Bretons, had warned her against Renée; and I wondered if, during her heavy drinking, she had not let slip some details about Christiane's death and this was being held over her. Finally I understood everything. Renée really was in control. Except that, by returning to Normandy, I had escaped her immediate attention; a wise opening gambit.

She had persuaded Françoise that it would be a good idea to invest her personal capital in the Cintra. The ruse was that the basement was unused and that it would make an ideal setting for a *tzigane* night club, which Françoise could operate under her guidance. I begged Françoise not to go through with the idea, but she insisted and used Renée's argument that in five years she would double her capital. Françoise received no encouragement from the *tzigane* community either. Boris and Katia, the incestuous brother and sister team who performed at the Tzarevitch, tried their best to discourage her. They even asked their deadly enemy Tania for her aid. Katia and Tania were worse than two rival cats in heat. One day Katia had pruned Tania's wig, which she had left unattended in the girls' dressing room, and tufts kept falling out onto the stage during her act. Tania swore she would kill Katia for that, but, putting her quarrel aside, she joined forces in the attempt to make Françoise see reason. Even Dimitri, the son of a Bulgarian Pope (orthodox priest in the east), another deadly enemy of Katia and who quit the Tzarevitch because of her to sing in the Monseigneur, joined the struggle, but to no avail. Françoise had taken a foolish decision and she was headstrong in her folly. The only thing standing in Renée's way was Jourdain the *notaire.* And Renée was just as headstrong as Françoise.

Without ever meeting Madeleine face to face Renée worked through Françoise to persuade the grandmother that, in view of her composed life at Ducey and in view of the apparent change for the better in Françoise's comportment compared with her erratic behaviour when she had left Paris for London, the time had come to lift the ward of court order which restricted Françoise's ability to govern her own capital. After the death of Christiane Madeleine was a broken woman and, at the age of 81, wanted only one thing, peace. She contacted the head of the family, Alexander Dior, who lived in Switzerland, and signed the decision of the *"conseil de famille"* which, in their opinion, considered Françoise capable of correctly occupying herself with her own affairs. Renée engaged an *avocat* to present the case before the civil tribunal and in due course, Françoise's ward of court order was retracted. She was on her own.

Renée immediately appropriated the greater part of Françoise's capital, leaving her enough pocket money to go drinking in the *tzigane* nightclubs each evening. No contract was ever signed, the money passed from hand to hand in a ladies' agreement. Renée was now totally in control. The first thing she did was to begin works on the Cintra; not to build the club in the basement, but to install two cold storage rooms in the restaurant kitchens, which she explained were necessary in order to cater for the flux of clients who would frequent the basement club.

As the months passed my "little jobs" for the RG became larger and larger and I found myself travelling between not only Belgium, but Holland, Germany, and Luxembourg; and in one instance to Africa, which nearly cost me my life. If national security in France has no rival anywhere in the world it is because, unlike the United States or Britain who rely on electronic intelligence gathering, Paris sticks to the good old time proven grass roots methods of using live agents in the field.

At first I was being tested with insignificant missions to see what I made of the jobs. Twice I had a rendezvous when suddenly I was approached, once in the metro and once in the street, by a very attractive girl who would strike up a conversation, eventually proposing that we might have a drink together somewhere. I have never had this kind of success in my entire life and the fact I had a meeting arranged each time can hardly be considered a coincidence. I never received any special instruction in my new trade; I was simply given an outline and told to get on with things myself. Amongst the marginal benefits, I was given a post office box number to where I could send any parking tickets or speeding fines which I might collect, and at the same time I had a telephone number to call in case I had any trouble in France. Outside France I was on my own, with no possibility of any help.

This curious occupation was as interesting as working with the vet but, one day towards the end of 1979, I was called to our usual meeting place in Avranches with my two friends.

We sat in the bar when one announced in a very serious tone, "I'm afraid we've got some very bad news for you." My insides turned over and I expected the worst. They continued, "The socialists are going to win the next presidential election." The next election was not due until the spring of 1981 and I could hardly see how that affected me; as a foreigner I did not have the right to vote, but they gave me the explanation. Although Valéry Giscard d'Estaing was the conservative President of the day, the situation was exactly the same as for my old school. The Tory government had started doing Wilson's dirty work for him two years before he had been elected. Giscard now started doing Mitterrand's dirty work for him long before he had been elected; and my old deportation order had been taken out of its drawer and was waiting for the day when the socialists would come to power in order to be executed.

They gave me the solution: stop being a marginal, find a regular job, start paying taxes and after at least a year as a worthy citizen things should go in my favour. Otherwise there was nothing they could do to help me. In eighteen months' time they would be working for a new minister. I had my back against the wall. If my deportation order had risen to the surface, Françoise was in the same boat. I went to Paris to explain the situation without giving her any detail as to the source of my information.

We took a terrace table at the Café de la Paix beside the Opéra and sat down in the weak sunshine to have an agreeable afternoon together. Françoise did not seem particularly concerned about our pending destiny. She was in the worst state that I had ever seen her, far worse than when she had swallowed the bleach in Jersey. She had aged well beyond her years and looked almost like a skeleton. Work on the basement club had ground to a halt because, as Renée explained, the architect had discovered a structural girder which had to be displaced before the works could properly begin. I was less convinced and decided to put Christiane's inverted cross to work as soon as I returned to Ducey. This was not going to solve my immediate problem of finding a regular job.

Françoise struck up a conversation with an American tourist at the table beside us and eventually took him to visit her future club. She had been reduced to picking up men in the street. I forgot all about her and concentrated on my own worries. Just as I had ordered another beer an ambulance forced its way through the heavy Parisian traffic with its blue light flashing and klaxon blaring. I remembered my own first aid certificates in a drawer back at Ducey and decided for my first honest job in France I would become an *"ambulancier"*.

CHAPTER 23

The Eighties

On my return to Ducey I explained to Sylvie my decision to enter the medical corps. An ambulance in France has no similarity whatsoever with the English counterpart, so the first thing to be done was to find out all about how I could enter the profession. Unlike in Britain where ambulance services are maintained by local authorities, terrestrial sanitary transports were for the greater part in the hands of small private companies. The same as with the farms, they were small family affairs. But, like the farms, they are now large inhuman factory style enterprises.

We went along to the ambulance company in Avranches, where I learnt the details. Anyone with the basic first aid certificates could become a driver, but, to work as a qualified ambulancier, a CCA certificate delivered by the Ministry of Health was obligatory. This involved a training course lasting three months. Two organisations covered my locality, the Order of St John in Caen and the university hospital of Pontchaillou in Rennes. They only held three *séances* each year. I contacted Caen but the inscription list was closed. At Rennes I was told the inscriptions were still open for the January 1980 *séance* but would be closing in two weeks. I had to hurry if I was going to make the deadline. This involved assembling all my diplomas, taking a medical exam at the *préfecture* to have my driving licence validated for "taxis, children's transports, and ambulances", suffering a whole series of vaccinations ranging from the BCG (tuberculosis vaccine) which I had missed at school, diphtheria, tetanus, polio, to a set of tropical vaccinations in case I had to handle freshly arrived immigrants; and, the most difficult to obtain, a certificate from a phthisiologist to certify I was free of tuberculosis. I could not find one anywhere in Normandy or Brittany who could take me immediately. Finally I found one at the hospital at Corbeil-Essonnes which covers Milly. I handed in my dossier with only one day to spare.

After my visit to Corbeil I called in to see Françoise, but back in Paris things were going from bad to worse. I had completely forgotten to put Christiane's inverted cross to work. Françoise was in a terrible state and in order to satisfy her sexual appetite she had begun to pick up men in cinemas on the boulevards which specialised in pornographic films. She seemed totally oblivious to the fact that we were both candidates for a free ride to Calais. The only money in her pocket was whatever Renée decided she needed for her immediate needs. Some tears slipped from her eyes and I held her close to me. She confessed that she had made a mistake with Christiane and suggested we returned to Ducey and get married to take up our lives together where we had left off before her daughter's arrival. I explained that our Normandy no longer existed and that she would be unhappy there. I could hardly tell her that she no longer resembled the Françoise I had first met in London only fourteen years previously. I returned to Ducey wishing I had never taken the detour via Paris.

My rush to complete my dossier was followed by the

entrance exam. There were forty places in each *séance*; twenty were reserved for existing medical personnel, ten for unemployed persons registered at the ANPE (*Agence Nationale pour l'Emploi*), the French version of the labour exchange, leaving only ten places free for independent candidates. Early one foggy morning all the candidates were assembled at the fire station in Rennes, where we were obliged to carry sandbags and weights of various measures and, in varying arm positions, go up and down staircases while a fire officer recorded our efforts. In the afternoon we were ushered into the hospital amphitheatre for the written exams. This dates back to the Napoleonic era, when hardly anyone in France spoke French. The Normans had their *patois*, the Bretons spoke Brezhoneg, the Alsatians spoke their version of German, and so it was with the Alps, the Basques, and all the other provinces which go to make up modern day France. To work for a state diploma you had to prove a certain mastery of the language in the name of national unity. A lot of the Emperor's laws are still in operation today and this was the only point which worried me, my rudimentary knowledge French.

My French could not have been all that bad because three weeks later I received a letter informing me that out of the hundred or so candidates for the ten free places I had to present myself at 9am on Monday 7th January, 1980, for my registration into the *"Ecole des Ambulanciers"*, on the second floor of the nursing school at the university hospital of Pontchaillou, Rennes. I became part of the hospital and was given a room at the end of the corridor which housed the student nurses. Our *séance* was divided into four groups of ten, each following different activities in the general schedule, only meeting up at midday in the hospital staff canteen. We had classes during the day where we were taught not only first aid but motor mechanics, map reading, and the complicated paper work involved in a social security where you paid for treatment first and were reimbursed much later. On three different weeks we were farmed out to various ambulance firms close to home to learn the job first hand, while during the other weeks we were used as slave labour in the hospital to accustom us to handling sick people. I did reanimation which involved many road accidents and suicides, the old folks' home, where I learnt to dress a senior citizen in one swift movement, and maternity.

Our evenings were free except twice a week for the maternity and those who worked with the fire brigade, whose main experience always seemed to arrive at night. I was up in front of the hospital disciplinary committee twice for unruly behaviour but, apart from that, in the *séance* everyone present were fairly ordinary rural characters, there were no true adventurers present. So I teamed up with three African girls I sometimes worked with in reanimation and who lived on my floor. They were already qualified nurses but were specialising for the operating theatre anaesthetics diploma. They had no car so I used to drive them to the university residence on the other side of town where there was a heavy African presence. That was real fun and it reminded me of Nairobi, where I had done a small job for my friends. I had no time free to swot up on my lessons like the others but, as the last week approached when we would be having our final exams, I had no particular doubts about my capacity as an *ambulancier*. Only one thing upset everything. I received a phone call from Françoise announcing her impending arrival in Rennes.

I duly met her off the Goéland, the express train from Paris to Brittany, and she settled in at the hotel du Guesclin which used to be situated just off the avenue Jean Janvier, near the station on the opposite side of town to the hospital. From then on I gave my canteen tickets to a Lebanese student nurse, who looked as if she appreciated them, and took all my meals at the du Guesclin. Françoise's objective was to destabilise me during the exams which she hoped I would fail and return to her. As usual she rose late in the mornings, we had lunch at the hotel together, and then I would leave her with Bibi, one of the African girls, who was in bed with a cold, while I took my turn at the exams. She had really made an effort in her appearance and could easily pass off as the Françoise I had always known in the past. The girls taking part in the *séance* who, during three months, had all declined my invitations for an evening out, all stood with their mouths agape as Françoise passed along the corridor between Bibi's room and the communal kitchen where she made some tea to keep her patient warm.

The Friday afternoon was nothing but tension. The results were to be posted on the notice board at any time and everyone was nervously milling about in the corridor. I sat with Françoise on the end of Bibi's bed while they chatted about witchcraft in Africa. Françoise sensed that she needed some real spiritual help and I remembered that I had completely forgotten Christiane's cross again. Bibi gave Françoise the address of an excellent *marabout* who just happened to be her cousin who lived in Paris and I silently wished her good luck. Word went up that the results had been posted so I joined the throng in the corridor. Out of forty candidates, I had come third. I later found out that I had really come first but the administration did not want to hold my unruly behaviour up as a good example to the others, so I had been demoted. We kissed Bibi goodbye, I collected my belongings from my room before handing in the key, drove a disappointed Françoise to the station, then drove back to Ducey to await my certificate to arrive in the post.

I found a job with a local ambulance firm and life began to be fun again. I rediscovered all the farms which I had missed so much, but now things were different. Sometimes it was heart breaking. The old folk always broke down crying when we arrived. This is because in the olden days, for granny in her bed beside the chimney, going to the hospital was always a one way trip. For the journey they insisted on dressing up in their Sunday best even though they knew they were going to be undressed as soon as they arrived at their destination. I quickly discovered the reason for the intensive training. At the time the emergency service known as the SAMU (*Service d'Aide Médicale Urgente*) did not exist. Most of the rural doctors were the wrong side of sixty-five and when the ambulance arrived we were expected to perform miracles. Half of the time the regulations were not respected and very often I was out alone without a chauffeur. I managed to make a mess of my very first emergency call. I hurtled through the countryside at full speed, pulled up at the cottage hospital, unloaded the stretcher and asked the *surveillant*, (French equivalent of a ward sister, male or female),

"OK, where is he?"

"What do you mean, where is he? It's you who's supposed to be bringing him in."

"Oh, OK, don't go away, I'll fetch him for you," and I hurtled off again.

I had mixed him up with a transfer which was on my order sheet for a later call.

One day I went home for lunch and was bubbling over with excitement. Sylvie was impatient for the news.

"*Cherie*, I've just saved a life. *Cherie*, I've just saved a life."

I kept it up all through the meal but the job quickly became a routine, exciting as it was. After six months I would come home for lunch and instead of saying, "*Cheri*e, I've just save a life," I'd say, "Another one sodded me up this morning."

By now there was some real trouble in Paris. Some more work had been done at the Cintra but, again, not on the basement club. The restaurant had been rewired and fitted out. The money was beginning to run out. In order to have some pocket money Renée had persuaded Françoise to mortgage the presbytery. In 1970, it had cost the equivalent of £9,000, a tidy sum in the day. But in 1980, Françoise was prepared to accept only £2,000, because, as Renée explained, it would be an easy sum to repay once the club was operational. I immediately knew this was the end of the presbytery but Renée had not won the match yet. After dipping Christiane's cross in the holy water in the *"bénitier"* just inside the church, while I recited Matthew 3.12, "Whose fan is in his hand, and he will thoroughly purge his floor, and gather his wheat into the garner; but he will burn up the chaff with unquenchable fire." I placed the cross on the appropriate page in the Bible which I then took back to the garage, where I laid it in the dust beneath my now unreadable inscription before lighting the remains of a black candle which had fallen beneath the cider press. From now on Renée could do her worst, her rendezvous with the Devil had been reserved.

For my part, my own troubles were just about to begin. At six am one morning the *gendarmerie* arrived at the presbytery in force, complete with a police dog. The previous year there had been a hold-up at the Credit Agricole bank in nearby St-Hilaire-du-Harcouët which had gone wrong, resulting in the deaths of two cashiers. The press had recently published a fairly detailed description of the movements of the bank robbers during the day before their hold-up. They were a man and woman who had taken the motorway from Belgium to Paris, picking up two Dutch hitchhikers who they had left on the outskirts of Paris before continuing on to Normandy. This just about fitted my own movements after one of my "little jobs" for my friends. The *gendarmerie* was convinced Sylvie and me were the authors.

They gave the presbytery a thorough search and, unfortunately, discovered a store of explosives which I had made for the FLB and a gun in my bedside cabinet, which corresponded exactly to the one used in the robbery. I spent the day at the *gendarmerie* being fingerprinted and photographed, the gun and the explosives were sent to Caen for examination, I was released in the early evening and Sylvie was left out of everything. This came about because on the 15th March, while I was living at the hospital in Rennes, a 7 kilo bomb comprising mostly of aluminium powder was discovered near Plogoff, which was going to be the site of a future nuclear project. An informer had tipped them off that I had begun to use metals in my explosives so they thought they had a lead on the Plogoff affair. But, tough luck for the *gendarmerie*, the explosives they had found at the presbytery were all based on magnesium. The story in the press about Bonnie and Clyde coming from Belgium was simply an invented pretext to bust the presbytery which the informer, knowing of my movements, must have slipped them; and the gun was nothing more than an unlucky coincidence on my part. The St Hilaire hold-up was never elucidated but I suddenly found myself shouldering the blame.

Sylvie and I decided it was time to get married, so we handed in our dossier at the town hall. Normally in France eleven days' notice is required for a marriage, but in those days a French citizen marrying a foreigner required thirty days. On top of that, permission from the local *"procurer"*, the public prosecutor, was also required. Needless to say, we received a phone call from the town hall saying permission had been refused. We immediately left the remaining dog in the charge of a close friend in the village and were on the boat for Dover that same night. We stayed at my parents' place in Dagenham and the next day we explained the situation to the registrar at the Barking office. After accomplishing all the formalities we were married by permission of His Grace, the Archbishop of Canterbury, by special licence on the 7th July and were on the boat back to Calais after a quick drink in the Matapan pub with Sylvie's witness, Stan Pulfer, who had once been a guard at Tyndall's National Front HQ at Excalibur House (also acting as election agent for the NF at Dagenham and who had visited us a few times at Ducey), and my witness, my mother. On returning to Ducey we had our marriage certificate translated by an authorised expert, then sent the copy to the *préfecture* for transcription. Everything was now in order.

The *gendarmerie* and the *juge d'instruction* dealing with the explosives did not appreciate our rapid marriage and, what with Françoise mortgaging the presbytery, we decided our days in Normandy were completely over. One of Sylvie's brothers lived in Corbeil-Essonnes and just by chance a small apartment immediately opposite his house was vacant, so we left Normandy for the Essonne. My Bible with Christiane's cross found a new abode in the garage attached to our apartment, which was bigger than the entire flat.

An ambulance in Paris has absolutely nothing in common with the service in the countryside and I was kept more than busy, far too busy compared with the pay, but the job is a vocation, either you like it or it is better to quit. I liked it. Shortly after our arrival in Corbeil I was summoned to Avranches by the *juge d'instruction*. The *juge*, the *greffier* and myself bundled into a small car driven by a *gendarme* and we set off to a deserted beach at the Bec d'Andaine on the mainland opposite Mont St Michel, where some army artificers from Caen were waiting to fire my explosives. Fortunately they must have grown damp while they were in store at Caen, because instead of the God almighty bang which once woke the entire town of Milly la Forêt one night while I was testing them in the forest and which provoked the rumour of a gas stove exploding the next day, their miserable performance destroyed my reputation as an able bodied extremist. The artificers recorded an ignition speed of 7,000 metres per second, which was the minimum if I was to be convicted of something. We were driven back to Avranches; I signed the report, and then went back to Corbeil.

Just by chance I stumbled upon Agnes Rampelberg. She was the widow of a director in the textile firm of Marcel Boussac, the "King of Cotton" and old friend of Christian Dior. Her brother Charles had once been a champion cyclist, winning a silver medal at the 1932 Los Angeles Olympics. He was riding as a sprint cyclist in Australia when the war broke out so he was stranded on the other side of the world when hostilities began. On one bad fall he injured his head on the wing nut of his front wheel and his performance rapidly deteriorated. Undeterred, he made his fortune in Australia running a French delicatessen, which was greatly appreciated by the Aussies. On his return to France he started a company with his brother, the artist

Emile Rampelberg, in the rue Mogador in Paris, where Emile created the designs for printed tissues while Charles travelled as a salesman presenting Emile's works to textile companies in South America and Spain. They became unbelievably rich, but Charles, champion as he was, always forced himself to the limit. Very often he would drive from Paris to Spain twice a week, in the days before the motorways were built, using the *routes nationales*. On one such trip during a particularly hot summer he suffered a severe cerebral congestion.

When Agnes introduced me to him he was a diabetic vegetable, rotting in the incurable section of the dreaded Paris asylum, the Sainte Anne. He sat in a courtyard where the sun never shines, gazing into space and surrounded by a variety of inmates, ranging from a mad genius who could recite *Pi* to the value of over forty points and was capable of solving the most complicated calculations in his head in just a few seconds, to an imbecile who rocked back and forth on a manhole cover all day. Agnes was heartbroken. Apart from his personal fortune, Charles possessed a studio in Le Lavandou on the Mediterranean coast, a thirteen roomed apartment in the luxury boulevard Exelmans in the 16e *arrondissement* of Paris, and his hacienda not far from Milly la Forêt. The plan was to install him in his hacienda while I became his gentleman's gentleman. Sylvie agreed and we went with Agnes to visit Charles's villa.

The building was in its own grounds of one hectare, completely surrounded by high hedges and trees. A Spanish gardener came from a nearby village from time to time to keep the garden in perfect condition. My pay was fantastic, three times what I would be earning in an ambulance, plus all the household expenses and food on top. The building itself was dominated by a large sitting room with a log fire at one end, an

American open kitchen at the other end, a glass conservatory on one side and two bedrooms on the opposite side. The bathroom also gave onto the sitting room and a third bedroom was in a small corridor by the front door. We could have had a daily maid if we wished but, not wishing to appear greedy, Sylvie said she would take care of everything about the house. There was no day off and the job was 24 hours a day, seven days a week. What did I care? We were totally independent; Sylvie was the mistress of the house, and I looked after Charles as if he had been my own grandfather. On top of everything there was a swimming pool in the garden beside the conservatory. Agnes and Emile were happy for their brother, Sylvie was happy, Charles was happy to find his old hacienda again, and I was happy to find a lifestyle similar to my former days at the presbytery. The only person who was upset was Françoise. Renée had decided to sell the Cintra.

The entire masquerade about creating the *tzigane* nightclub in the basement was nothing more than her means of extracting the cash from Françoise which she needed to carry out the necessary modernisations required in order to sell up. Françoise was devastated. Renée fobbed her off with a story about keeping the cash after the sale to buy something better where they would earn even greater money in the near or distant future.

On the 10th May, François Mitterrand was duly elected as president of the French republic. Fortunately for me, my trial had been fixed for the 2nd June, which meant my dossier had been treated well before the new government could interfere with things. But if ever I needed my friends from the RG, I needed them now. On the Tuesday afternoon I took my place at the bar of the *Tribunal de Grand Instance* at Avranches when called and waited while the formalities were completed. I was accused of *"fabrication and detention of engines explosive and incendiare,"* along with *"possession d'une arme de 4e catégorie sans autorisation."* When the judge asked for an explanation for the explosives I said I was making fireworks for the 14th July, Bastille Day. I said Sylvie, coming from a large family, had thirty-two nephews and nieces so it was cheaper to make my own. The judge informed me the state had the monopoly on the production of powder. I was guilty of tax evasion which was the realm of the customs. Concerning the firearm, I told the tribunal there were several jealous husbands about in Avranches and I was simply taking some elementary precautions. It brought the whole courtroom down in laughter. The judge gave me a ticking off and gave me two years suspended for two years. The case was over.

Outside in the courtyard the captain of the brigade of *gendarmes* threw his kepi to the ground, kicked it and said in his entire career it was the first time he had ever heard the prosecutor actually defending the prisoner. I was free to return to Corbeil and the hacienda near Milly. Before leaving Avranches I gave my friends in the RG a quick visit to thank them.

As promised, shortly after the new *Ministère de l'Interieur* had taken office I was called to Corbeil town hall concerning a social enquiry on my character. I was informed I had a deportation order out in my name but, considering my marriage, my job, and that I was paying my taxes regularly, the town hall sent in a favourable report. That was the last I was to hear about the affair. My deportation order was finally revoked in December 1983. Françoise must have had a similar enquiry but I have no idea how she fared. All I know is that she was now desperate. Madeleine stuck to her guns and although she permitted Françoise to live at the apartment in the square, she refused any material aid as far as money was concerned.

Françoise was standing on her own; the only valid solution was to remarry. She was going crazy, and contacted her old friend Jacques de Ricaumont at the *Association de Noblesse*. In the sorry condition in which she found herself any remarriage into the aristocracy was out of the question. She was fifty and looked sixty. All the available aristocrats were being snapped up by the younger beautiful girls, most of whom held their own family titles to begin with. Françoise was an outsider. In order to have the money for one last aesthetic operation and buy some new clothes, she sold the presbytery in Ducey. Deducting the mortgage and the unpaid instalments with interest accumulated, she received roughly the equivalent of £25,000 pounds. Abandoning the idea of the French aristocracy she toyed with the idea of remarrying with an Englishman and signed on with the Paris branch of the Conservative party. She made a small collection of pen friends in Britain but, after several abortive trips to visit various contacts throughout the British Isles, the idea fell flat.

At about the same time the six year concession on Christiane's pigeon-hole in the Columbarium at the Père Lachaise expired. Françoise had no money to renew the lease and Madeleine had been staunchly against a cremation from the very start. Coupled with the fact Christiane had been disposed of without any religious ceremony, she refused to have anything further to do with her remains. According to the cemetery records, at the expiry date Christiane's ashes were exhumed and dumped into the common grave along with the tramps and unidentified deceased which had been recovered within the Parisian city limits. The cross which Françoise had given me to place with Christiane's ashes followed the girl into the pit.

During this time Charles Rampelberg died. The family let us have a holiday in the studio at Le Lavandou but, after Easter, we were obliged to return to our small flat in Corbeil. I took a job with a local ambulance firm, a typical small enterprise with one CCA, namely me, two chauffeurs, the boss doing some driving when we were busy, and his wife doing the accounts. There were seven such firms in Corbeil at the time. Today only one covers the entire Corbeil, Evry, Ris Orangis, and surrounding district, exactly the same set-up as in the farms. Sylvie was now expecting the arrival of our son and, being unbelievably thrifty, she had saved enough ready cash from our time at the hacienda to permit me to spend a lengthy period on the dole in order to look after her. We found a house to rent on the higher slopes of Corbeil and moved in waiting for my Jasmine to arrive. At the last minute Jasmine turned out to be Christophe. The echography was still unreliable at the time. Comfortably on the dole, I changed the nappies at night while Sylvie could have a decent sleep.

Françoise was at the end of her tether. In one last desperate attempt she joined Jacques Chirac's conservative party, the RPR. It was here she met Count Hubert Georges de Mirleau. At the time Mirleau was working in reassurance, the strange complicity between the insurance companies where they reassure each other's risks in the event of being hit with a heavy payout. His job involved frequent business trips to Germany, where he spoke the language fluently. He also spoke perfect English with next to no accent, whereas Françoise had kept a French accent you could cut with a knife. Mirleau was an officer of the exclusive *Cercle Montherlant*, consisting of a complete collection of princes, ambassadors and aristocrats, meeting regularly at dinner-conferences in diverse *chateâux* and museums, where the orators would discuss matters of historical and social interest. Homosexuality was an underlying interest amongst the members.

Although he was single, Mirleau had a girlfriend who lived in the rue Tilsitt, near the Belgian embassy facing the Arc de Triomphe. His girlfriend was rich but, although Mirleau himself was only earning about £2,000 a month in his insurance, he had the title; and his mother lived in the expensive boulevard Suchet, overlooking the Bois de Boulogne.

According to Françoise, her version of events was that a) Mirleau met her; b) He fell deeply in love with her; c) He dumped his girlfriend; and d) He married Françoise as soon as possible.

My own version, and I might be wrong but, knowing Françoise, I doubt it, is that a) She met him; b) In view of Madeleine's colossal fortune and the fact she was now 86 he considered Françoise to be a good investment; c) He told his girlfriend to be patient for a while; and d) He married Françoise as soon as possible.

Whatever happened, they were married. Using the remainder of Françoise's money from the sale of the presbytery they took out a small apartment in the rue de Varenne, near the Prime Minister's residence. Right from the very beginning Françoise put her foot down concerning Mirleau's absences in Germany for his insurances. She made him leave his fairly well paid job and from then on he was totally dependent on her whims.

Shortly after their marriage Françoise and Mirleau

received a visit from Martin Webster, who had broken away from Tyndall and the National Front, founding his own party, "Our Nation". In order to have some funds he managed to scrounge £1,000 from Françoise, who deeply regretted the loss of such a sum from the household budget. But she gave it to Webster simply to save face and maintain the illusion that the Mirleaus were living in the height of luxury. Notwithstanding the money from Françoise and some initial support from Denis Pirie, "Our Nation" floundered and never managed to get off the ground. The money from the presbytery was rapidly depleting and something drastic had to be done.

Their days at the rue Varenne were coming to an end.

CHAPTER 24

And the Devil takes the hindmost

Françoise and Mirleau hardly made a happy couple. In all outward appearances they presented the aspect of a minor aristocratic family, without imposing themselves as Françoise would once have done in the past. At home, when there is no hay in the stable the horses fight amongst themselves. There was no question of divorce; they would have both been high and dry and they relied on each other for mutual support. Mirleau confessed to me that their destiny relied upon two old ladies; I presume he meant their respective mothers.

My own situation was not famous either, because although I had a fairly well paid job in the ambulances, things could have been better. When we lived in lower Corbeil there was a bank immediately opposite our apartment and I would often watch as the armoured van stood parked in the street below while the conveyers would take their sacks of money to and fro between their vehicle and the bank. After my bad experience in Normandy, bank robbery was out of the question and the conveyers were mean looking guys who carried guns. This vision haunted me and just as I was wondering how I might obtain a few of the sacks for myself I heard a very interesting story on the BBC news. A conveyer in London had disappeared with his van containing a quarter of a million pounds and, although the van had been recovered, the conveyer and the cash had completely vanished off the face of the earth. The solution was so obvious I wondered how I could have missed it. My plan was to start off small in some cheap security firm, then work my way up the ladder before finally finding myself working in an armoured van. I went along to the ANPE to enquire about the trade. There was an ad on display inviting candidates for a training course in security leading to the coveted IGH2 diploma, security in skyscrapers. I noted the address and immediately wrote off.

Within a few days I received a reply inviting me to a selection reunion somewhere in Paris where the course would be explained and the candidates would be examined to test their ability to follow the course, which would last for three months. I sat in a hall with a whole host of candidates where we watched a short film projection. After the film had ended we had to answer questions concerning our own personal interpretation of the film. One week later I received the notification that I should present myself on a certain Monday morning at a *château* just outside Meaux, deep in the countryside to the north-east of Paris. On arrival, I discovered I had hit the big time first go. The training course was organised by the ACDS, the biggest rival in Paris to Brink's and the SPS. I planned that after one year of behaving myself I would ask for my transfer to the armoured van division.

The training course was tough going. When we were not in class learning the theory of fire fighting and the complicated safety regulations which cover high rise buildings we were out in the snow, learning how to throw a rolled hosepipe so that it opens at first go and how to roll it up again correctly so that it opens again on the following throw, along with the fixed positions of each fire fighter on the terrain, and the specific duties of each member of a team of three. We learnt how to handle fire extinguishers and how to cope with the five different categories of fire which go to make up a good blaze. After that it was learning the general structure of a building and how to be at home in front of any kind of security risk which might present itself during our future careers.

My first post, however, was not in a high rise building, but as a receptionist at the IBM head office in the place Vendome, Paris. The other members of the security staff were all perfectly bilingual and had the presentation of being high class butlers rather than fire fighters. My first week got off to a bad start. The *"Président-directeur-général"* was a decent enough guy called Lemonnier. But his number two, Pierre Barazer, was thoroughly fed up with me from the very beginning. Not being a very good physiognomist I can just about recognise Father Christmas in his working uniform. IBM company policy required all employees to wear an identity badge and I always stopped Barazer at least five times a day. There was just something about him which I failed to recognise all the time. In the end he avoided me. On the whole IBM was not so bad and the pay was excellent because whenever someone in the security failed to turn up on one of the other nine IBM sites scattered here and there about Paris, I was often called upon to replace them by doing a second shift in my day, something which is illegal under French labour laws.

Sylvie decided we now had enough money to buy our own home, the apartment where we have now lived for the past twenty-six years, but I was still thinking about the armoured vans. Two months before I asked for my transfer we opened an account at the HSBC in Brussels in Sylvie's name. Then, one month beforehand, I applied at the Argentine consulate for a long term visa. Unlike the Great Train Robbers, I was not going to be found sitting on the end of my bed with a pile of unopened bags underneath my feet when the police called.

Just before Christmas the great day arrived. I went to the ACDS stores to hand in my receptionist's costume in exchange for a conveyer's leather jacket, an identity medal, a gun holster and a written permit signed by the prefect of Paris authorising me to carry a loaded firearm in public. On my first day I was allocated to an experience team who roughly explained the job and said I would learn as we went along. The quartermaster gave me a Smith and Wesson 357 magnum and I helped the lads loading up the bags who showed me how to arrange them in order in the strong room of the van. The doors were fastened and we drove off. At the end of the first day I could hardly believe my bad luck; the van was half empty with bags of cheques, courier between the banks, and coins which weighed a ton. The next day was no better. One day we drove over eighty kilometres simply to deliver a credit card to a distant bank. After two weeks I discovered I had wasted an entire year of my life, the vans were always very nearly empty; it is no wonder the firm finally went bankrupt shortly after I had left.

Just as with Eddy Bartram's red Mercedes, Françoise took a certain inspiration after my own activities. One day I stumbled upon Françoise and Mirleau while I was delivering some bags to the Société Générale at the Opéra. I let Mirleau handle my Smith and Wesson and Françoise decided it suited him to have a revolver in his hand. She obliged him to acquire one illicitly shortly afterwards. My initial contract as a conveyer was for three months so as its conclusion approached I decided not to renew it. My boss said with the coming Easter holiday a lot of the effective would be off on vacation so if I could remain an extra few weeks he would give me a small bonus on my final pay slip. The armoured vans must have been one of the greatest deceptions in my whole life.

I had not neglected my daily ritual concerning Christiane's inverted cross. It lived in its Bible on top of the Norman wardrobe in our bedroom at our new apartment, a direct link with Ducey. And now I had placed a magic stone on top, which I had found one day on the summit of the evil Mont Dol. Anyone can make a magic stone. It takes a year and a lot of perseverance but it's one of those oddities of nature which is guaranteed to work in the same way as the simple experiments which I had withheld from Françoise in the past. When I decided it was time to remove the stone I threw it into the Seine accompanied by a demonic curse. At the same time, Renée died.

Françoise and Mirleau were desperate for some money. Françoise had once told me while we were living in Ducey that if one day she was ever ruined by unforeseen circumstances she would become a *"dame de companie"* to a rich elderly person, in much the same way as I had become Charles' gentleman's gentleman. I can only presume she had realised her dream. They moved out of the rue Varenne and took up lodging with a rich old girl who lived in the square des Ecrivains Combattants Morts pour la France, in the 16e *arrondissement* overlooking the Bois de Boulogne and giving on to the boulevard Suchet where Mirleau's mother lived. The name of the square is so long the post office simply refers to it as the square des Ecrivains.

Mirleau had decided Françoise was entitled to some kind of compensation from Renée, even though no written agreement had ever been signed between them. A case was prepared, ready to be presented in civil justice. In despair Renée hanged herself, exactly as Christiane had hanged herself the night before Renée had started to wear her accursed ring.

I removed Christiane's cross from between its biblical pages, dipped it in the holy water in the curious parish church of Evry, which was built by the Knights Templar and is oriented north/south instead of the usual east/west, and returned it to its habitual box on Sylvie's dressing table, where it has remained ever since. The Devil had taken two souls and was satisfied with his work. Renée had been kind enough to take the second place in the triangle and now there remained only a third, but who was it to be?

After leaving the armoured vans I was in for a long period on the dole. My friends were suddenly kept busy and my "little jobs" abroad multiplied. My own pact with the Devil had only just begun in earnest. Sylvie was none too happy about the situation because, with our son just starting school, she was obliged to stay at home for most of the time instead of joining me on my trips. After a well-deserved holiday on the Ile de Ré on the Atlantic coast there was a pause in my activities and I found a job with another ambulance firm near Evry. This was to be very short lived. A war in the Persian Gulf was brewing and in view of my experience handling explosives and clandestine activities in general, someone suggested I should work for an Israeli firm specialising in security based at Orly airport. I was signed on and spent the following months either stripping down aircraft bound for Tel Aviv and Jerusalem looking for bombs or sitting in an obscure corner of an airline office in Paris waiting for some trouble to start. The war was over in record time so I returned to the ambulances.

Françoise had maintained a conversational contact with Diana although she was no longer living in Greenwich and had moved to God's waiting room, Eastbourne, to be nearer to her two friends from the Front, John Tyndall and Denis Pirie, who had both retired to the Brighton and Hove district. During one telephone call which Françoise had made, urgently seeking some reassuring comfort, Diana could hear Mirleau cursing and screaming at Françoise in the background, while Françoise half confessed, "I'm being punished for what I did to my daughter." This was meaningless to Diana until I explained the situation well over ten years later.

Another of my own activities which had inspired Françoise was my book with which she had made so much easy money. She now began to oblige Mirleau, much against his will, to write a book himself. I can recognise every phrase in the book right down to the cover design; she had first seen it in one of my *Man, Myth and Magic* magazines in Ducey.

During this time I had the job of returning a young apprentice cook from Evry hospital, where he had received treatment for some bad scalding butter burns, to the *auberge* where he worked on the banks of the Seine at Draveil. I immediately fell in love with the building in its own wooded grounds, a small restaurant with a log fire at one end of the room, and a jetty for tying up visiting pleasure craft on the river. I might just as well have been beside a river in the middle of the Norman countryside. This *auberge* had once been a favourite haunt of the writer and journalist Edmond de Goncourt, after whom the prestigious literary prize has been named, and who came here in the company of the equally famous writer

Alphonse Daudet, who lived nearby. My forty-fifth birthday was approaching and I decided to hold a small reception here. In October the autumn leaves would be falling from the trees, in the evening a fog would be rising from the river, a log fire would make the ideal setting and it would also be the season for wild boar in chestnut and mushroom sauce. What more could I wish for?

Although I was born on the 29th, the original night for my reception was fixed for the 25th October, the night of St. Crispin, Henry V's battle of Agincourt. Françoise asked that it be put back to the 26th and, on seeing her at the table, I very quickly realised the reason behind her request. I arrived early with Sylvie, our seven year old son Christophe and one of Sylvie's nephews, in order to make sure everything was in place correctly. I cannot remember exactly how many were present but everyone arrived either one by one or in couples. As he was the senior politician present I placed Claude Cornilleau at the head of the table. Claude was the leader of the ill-fated PNFE (Le Parti Nationaliste Français et Européen), the most extreme of the extreme right wing movements of the day. He was accompanied by his son. Beside Claude sat Stan Pulfer, the National Front agent from Dagenham, and beside Stan were Françoise and Mirleau. Count Michel Roch Faci sat beside Mirleau. Faci was one of the last true adventurers. He had accompanied Bruno Renoult, long before the days when Bruno had dug up Soviet generals, in their misadventures in Brittany. His latest escapade was to have organised a group of mercenaries to fight alongside Saddam Hussein in the first Gulf war. A few years later he was to accompany Bruno and myself on the *"banc des accusés"* at Saintes in the million franc bank fraud. Bruno and Faci each spent a year behind bars with the remainders of their sentences commuted to suspensions, while my own condemnation suffered a vice of procedure which, under French law, invalidated the judge's sentence, rendering it inapplicable.

I sat with Sylvie opposite Françoise and Mirleau and the remainder of the table, which took up the entire length of the room, was made up of members of Sylvie's immediate family. It was during the meal which followed that I discovered Françoise's secret concerning her health. I had seen enough of her cases while in the ambulances. She took an aperitif before the meal and drank absolutely nothing else during the rest of the evening. She was obviously on dialysis. The 25th must have been her day for treatment.

As a birthday gift Mirleau presented me with a copy of his book which had just been published: *"La démocratie, est elle une fatalité?"* (Democracy, is it a fatality?) A lot of it is based on a pamphlet of which I have forgotten the title, written by Good Borisz, and which is now in the Vatican library. I know it off by heart because originally it was a lecture which he once delivered at the Université Populaire, Vevey, in Switzerland. I typed his copy for him on dictation at Ducey and it was based on the Swiss philosopher, Jacob Burckhardt's theory that history is repetitive. I can see Françoise in every single line.

In connection with books, I informed Françoise for the first time that my *Twice Born* had been pirated and made into a film. She made no comment and had the same troubled look as she had shown at Ducey when the cash had finally run out. I began explaining how I would like to attack whoever had pretended it was their work, but Claude saved the day by saying I should forget it because the studios already have these eventualities written into their budget and I would never win. The topic changed to the *Cercle Montherlant*. In all it was a wonderful evening beside the log fire inside the *auberge* and the Seine fog amongst the trees outside. Just after midnight everyone went their separate ways except Françoise and Mirleau, whose red Mercedes inspired by Eddie Bartram needed a push because the freezing night air had flattened the battery. They had a nice car but no cash for the upkeep.

It would be some time before I was to see Françoise and Mirleau again. I was just returning from Germany after a small job for my friends when I received an invitation for an evening dinner at the *Cercle de l'Union Interallié* in Paris. This club was originally founded in 1917, after the entry of the United States into the Great War, in a building owned by Henri de Rothschild in the rue du Faubourg St Honoré, right next to the British embassy. The objective was for it to be a high class club for officers and dignitaries of the *"Triple Entente"*. Today it is made up of ministers, *avocats*, and diverse aristocrats. Mirleau, by cause of his title, was a member, but Françoise's secret was that the couple should make regular appearances at places such as this as part of her panoply, designed more to convince herself than anyone else that she went to make up part of something. She reminded me of the old ladies who waited until pension day to visit the hairdresser before taking up position in the Westminster Hotel in Nice. A flunky at the door insisted I left my shoulder bag at the cloakroom, which I reluctantly did. I had my camera and video gear inside and if ever it went missing there was enough on the cassettes to have created a diplomatic incident between France and Germany. Françoise's behaviour confirmed my suspicion she was on dialysis. On top of that she presented a terrible aspect and there were moments when I thought she was about to pass out. What

I never realised at the time was this was her way of saying goodbye to me. She knew she was dying. The very thing she feared the most had caught up with her. Her cancer phobia which had started with the death of the young *percepteur* in Ducey had finally won.

At the beginning of the following year I received a phone call from Mirleau. Françoise had died at a quarter to midnight on Wednesday 20th January, at the American Hospital at Neuilly sur Seine in the northern suburbs of Paris. She was only sixty years old, six years younger than I am today. He invited me for a dinner at the Cercle Montherlant, where the waiters and directors all presented their condolences to the distraught widower. Two weeks later Mirleau came to Evry for a meal with us where I gave him the few photographs and items which I had remaining of Françoise. Sitting on the sofa he told us how, towards the end, Françoise suffered from a delirium where she saw herself being consumed with flames in her bed. I could hardly tell him anything about the pact which she had made seventeen years previously with Christiane concerning their master the Devil. Someone had simply arrived to reclaim one of his own. The triangle had been completed.

Mirleau was far too hard up to give his wife the splendid Nordic cremation of which Françoise had always dreamt since the days in Ducey when she had come to venerate the Wagnerian gods in her attic chapel. Years after her death I learnt that Madeleine had taken pity on the daughter, with whom she had continuously quarrelled since the day when Françoise had discovered her true lineage, and had taken her funeral arrangements into hand. Françoise was buried with full Christian rites in the Leblanc family vault in the avenue Pacthod at the Père Lachaise